The Sayings And Doings Of The Celebrated Mrs. Partington: And Others Of The Family

Benjamin Penhallow Shillaber

THE

SAYINGS AND DOINGS

OF THE

CELEBRATED

MRS. PARTINGTON,

("*Relic*" *of Corporal P.P.*)

AND OTHERS OF THE FAMILY.

SECOND EDITION.

LONDON:

JAMES BLACKWOOD, PATERNOSTER ROW.

1854.

"There, shore enough, was a sight as froze my blood to calves-foot jelly. There was the soger cap and coat, as nateral as life, with the tompion atop. My heart come up into my mouth, so that I could have spit it out just as easy as not."—P. 12.

PREFATORY.

Mrs. Partington once declined an introduction to a party, because she did not wish to be introduced to any one she was not acquainted with. She needs no introduction now. In all parts of our own land, and over the sea, her name is familiar as a household word; and "as Mrs. Partington would say" forms a tributary clause to many a good story, or an apology for many a bad one; a smile attending the utterance of the name in evidence of its appreciation. But a preface, of course, is expected; and so, in the most gentle manner in the world, we will tell to you, reader, a little story about the origin of the Partington sayings, and why they were said, and why they are here collected. Perhaps you have guessed it all; but it is well to be certain.

In the first place, they were written, as the canine quadruped is said to have gone to church, for fun,—for the author's own amusement,—with a latent hope, however, half-indulged, that the big world, which the author very much loves and wishes to please, might see something in them at which to smile. He was modest in his hope, and hid himself behind an incognito, impenetrable, he thought, where he could see the effect of his mild squibs upon the public. The result pleased him, and he kept vigorously blazing away, unseen!—as much so as the simple bird that thrusts its head under a leaf and fancies itself unobserved!— until they have arisen to a magnitude that some people might deem respectable.

The origin and object of the Partington "sayings" being thus described, the motive for their collection shall be confessed. It is the hope that their author may make a little money on them. He is not so squeamish or pretending as to talk of public good, and public amusement, as his leading motives in the matter; but if these can be obtained through the publication, he will be most happy. The author confesses to certain pressing contingencies—by no means peculiar to him, however, among authors—that would be relieved by a generous return for his outlay of time; and that his pouch may take a more silvery hue from the circulation of his book, is a consummation devoutly, by him, to be wished.

This motive, so entirely original, for the publication of a book, the author has secured under the guarantee of his copy-right. There might be no necessity for this, where all the rest of the author tribe are writing and printing from higher motives; but he pleads selfishness, and, like the old lady in her variance with St. Paul, there is where he and they differ.

Some wiseacre has recently made a discovery, of what we have proclaimed from the outset, that the name of Mrs. Partington was not original with us—that Sydney Smith first gave it to the world. Most profound discoverer! But the *character* we claim as ours; and whether it had been embodied in Mrs. Smith, or Brown, instead of Mrs. Partington, would have been immaterial. Those sayings are *ours*, and we venture to affirm that Sydney Smith would not lay claim to them, from the fact that they were uttered by one of the same name as his heroine of the mop. Because, forsooth, he had spoken of Mrs. Partington's sweeping back the Atlantic with her broom, would he claim the illustrious PAUL, and the roguish ISAAC, and the jocose ROGER, and the great PHILANTHROPOS, and the poetical WIDESWARTH, as his progeny? We trow not, even though others might be found ready to do it for him.

The character has been drawn from life. The Mrs. Partington we have depicted, is no fancy sketch, and no Malaprop imitation, as some have thought, who saw in it nought but distorted words and queer sentences. We need no appeal to establish this fact. Mrs. Partington is seen everywhere, and as often without the specs and cap as with them.

CONTENTS.

CONTENTS.

BIOGRAPHY

OF

MRS. PARTINGTON,

RELICT OF P. P., CORPORAL.

PAUL PARTINGTON, whose name is immortalised by its association with that of the universal MRS. PARTINGTON, a portion of whose oracular sayings our book comprises, came from the old country, by water probably, somewhere in the early days of our then not very extensive civilisation. At that time people were not in the habit of putting everything into the papers, as they do now, when the painting of a front door, or the setting of a pane of glass, or the laying of an egg, is deemed of sufficient consequence for a paragraph ; much, therefore, of interest concerning the early history of his family is merely known by the faint light which tradition has thrown upon it.

A story has come down to us from remote time, through the oracular lips of the oldest inhabitants, that Paul was troubled in the old country by certain unpleasant and often-recurring reminders of indebtedness, yclept " bills," which were always, like a summer night, falling due, and certain urgently-pressing importunities, the which, added to a faith that was not too popular by any means, at last induced him to warily scrape together such small means as he could, and incontinently retire from metropolitan embarrassment to the comparative quiet of an emigrant's life, where he might encounter nothing more annoying than the howling of wolves or the yelling of savages, sweet music both when contrasted with the horror comprised in the words " PAY THAT BILL !" which had long distressed him. Here the voice of the dunner was done, and Paul, under his own vine and pine-tree, worshipped God and cheated the Indians, according to the dictates of his own conscience and the custom of the times.

B

The "*new house*," as the family mansion has been called for a century, to distinguish it from some *old* house that had at some previous time existed somewhere, was erected about the year ——, as is supposed, from the discovery of a receipted bill from Godfrey Pratt, for "Ayde in Rayse'g ye Nue Eddiffyce," which bears date as above, and likewise from the fact that a child was born to the erector of the new house the same year, which was duly chronicled in the ancient Bible, with other blessings, and the word "Howse" is distinctly to be traced among them.

The new house was a staunch piece of work, erected at a time when men were honest, and infused much of their own character into the work they put together; the beams of oak so sturdy, that Time, failing to make an impression upon them, gives up at last in despair. The house was intended as a garrison, and where the clapboards had chafed off were revealed the scarfed logs, denoting where the loop-holes were, and the leaden bullets, still left there, which Paul was wont to dig out with his knife, when a boy, and make sinkers of for his fishing-lines. Many a story that venerable house could tell of ancient warfare, of the midnight attack and gallant defence; but it never told a thing.

It was in this house that Paul Partington was born and grew, amid all the luxuries that the town of Beanville afforded, said town at that time consisting of five houses and a barn.

In this house he was married, the most momentous act of his life, as through the hymeneal gate came upon the world the dame whose name we are delighted to honour. We find upon the fly-leaf of a treatise on calcareous manures, yet sacredly treasured, the following memorandum, in the corporal's own writing, significant of the methodical habit of the man who shed, in after life, as far as a corporal's warrant could do it, undying glory upon his country:—"Married this day, January the 3, 1808, to Ruth Trotter, by Rev. Mr. Job Snarl. Forty bushels of potatoes to Widow Green."

There is a blending of bliss and business in this entry, that strikes one at the first glance. The record of the sale of the potatoes in the same paragraph announcing his marriage to Ruth, might signify to some that they were held in equal regard. But we see the matter differently. The purchase of Ruth and the sale of the potatoes were the two great events of that important 3d of January, and they naturally associated themselves. So you, madam, might associate the birth of your first-born, the most blissful moment of your life, with the miserable matter of the death of a lame duck or the blowing down of a pig-sty.

Of the courtship that preceded that marriage, we can say

nothing, except what we have gleaned by accident from the old lady herself. In rebuking the want of sincerity of devotion now-a-days, on the part of lovers, she once spoke of a time when *some one* would ride a hard-trotting horse ten miles every night, and back, for the sake of sitting up with her. But no name was mentioned.

Ruth Partington—born Trotter—came amid sublunar scenes several years before the nineteenth century commenced, consequently she is older than 1800. She was a child, by law, for eighteen years before she became a woman, and performed the duties "incumbered" upon her, as we have been informed by her, with great fidelity.

We should be false to our object—that of writing a true biography of Mrs. Partington—did we pretend that she was perfect. We would take this pen and inkstand, as well as they have served us in our need, and throw them in the grate, before we would make any such assertion. But we must say that we never heard she had an enemy, and Tradition—that grim old chap, that has so many bad things to say about people, and so few that are good—never said a word about it.

A kind heart has characterised Mrs. Partington from her childhood up, displayed in many ways. Her benevolence got far in advance of her grammar in her early days, and in her sayings at times are detected certain inaccuracies that some people are inclined to laugh at; but if they will stop a little, and see the yellow kernels of wisdom gleaming out through the thickly surrounding verbiage, they will raise their hats in grateful respect for the bounty afforded.

The domestic history of Mrs. Partington requires a nice pen to portray it, so full was it of delicate beauty and delightful incident. Marriage meant something in old times. It was no holiday affair, donned like a garment, to be regarded as worthless when the fashion changed. It grew out of no sickly sentiment, that had its existence in the yellow fever of a wretched romance, as unlike true life as a cabbage is to a rose; or the sere of autumn—a more fitting simile—to the vernal spring. It was a healthy, hearty, happy old institution in those days, was matrimony; and people jogged along together in the harness of its duties, as harmoniously as the right hand and the left, that help each other and yet don't seem to know it, so naturally is the service rendered—as if they were born to it. And as the right hand or the right eye sympathises with the left, so did the twain thus united sympathise. Duty and affection leaned upon each other, and inseparably strove to make the home hearth cheerful.

It became pleasure to carry the sweet drink to the thirsty man, in the field a mowing : or to bear the basket of luncheon to the woods where the red-browed man was chopping wood for winter; or to patiently hold the light in the long winter evenings, when the yokes were to be mended, or the harness repaired. And it became pleasure, when the goodman went to town, to stow his pockets with something nice for the wife at home—a new dress or a new apron—the remembrance of whose face would come to him when away, and hasten his departure back. It was that remembrance which prompted the mare into an urgent trot on the last mile home—though she couldn't see the necessity for it —and his eye looked brighter when he saw the cheerful face at the window, looking down the road, and shook his whip at it as it smiled at him, as much as to say, Let me get near you, and ————and what ? Ask the walls, and the bureau in the corner, and the buffet where the china was, or the milk-pans upon the dresser, what.

No jars occurred in a home that owned such a pair. Can the right hand quarrel with the left ? Can the left eye cast severe glances upon the right ? The home where a true marriage exists is blest, and the man who finds his domesticity cast in a mould such as we have described, may be called happy in the fullest sense of the blissful word.

It would have done all of us good to peep in upon fireside-scenes at the Partington mansion. The fire-place, with its wide and hospitable arms extended, looked like an incentive to population, having family capacity revealed in its huge dimensions. It was a brave idea of Seek Partyngetonne, and when he laid the corner-stone of the Beanville structure, he had visions of a posterity as numerous as the leaves of the sweet-briar bush that waved by his door. Alas! how were those visions verified, as a few generations saw the line of Seek diminishing, to find its end, at last, like the snap of a whip lash, in one little knot.

But those scenes ! It was the custom of the corporal, in the long nights of winter, to seat himself in the right corner of the old fire-place, while the dame occupied the other, and read, by the light of a mutton tallow candle, such literature as the house afforded. This was comprised in the family Bible, an old and massive volume that adorned the black bureau under the glass ; a copy of army tactics, presented to Paul by a revolutionary soldier ; and a copy of Dudley Leavitt's Almanac. These were read, by the light of mutton fat, aloud, while Mrs Partington pursued her knitting in the corner, nodding at times, perhaps, as the theme was dull or familiar ; but the smile always rewarded

Paul's effort to amuse her, as much as if he hadn't read the same things over and over a thousand times. The small, covered earthen pitcher kept time to his reading often, and sung and spluttered upon the coals between the old-fashioned dog-and-irons, as if a spirit were within, struggling to throw off the cover that restrained it, and escape. Regularly, as the hand of the old bull's-eye watch on the nail over the mantel-piece denoted the hour of nine, was the book laid by, and the mug taken from the fire, and its steaming contents poured into the white earthen bowl upon the table, which sent up a vapour that rolled upon the dark walls like a fragrant cloud, and made the room redolent with the fume of the " mulled cider" that smoothed the pillow of Paul.

Mrs. Partington, as the presiding genius of these scenes, shed the radiance of her presence over the circle, as the sunflower claims eminence in a garden of marigolds. Her sage voice was heard in wise counsel; and in giving the news of who was sick, or dead, or about to be married, or wasn't about to be married, but ought to be, she was at home.

It would be impossible, in the small space allotted us, to describe all the virtues of Mrs. Partington. It were best to make an aggregate of good, and call it all hers. The herbs that adorned the garret walls in innumerable paper bags, were not gathered for herself; the balm-of-gilead buds and rum, that occupied their position in the buffet, were not prepared for her; but at the first note of distress from a neighbour her aid was ever ready. She was the first who was sent for on important occasions, when goodwives must be wakened from their beds at midnight; and to this day half the population at Beanville speak of the benevolent face that bent over them in the first moments of their struggle with existence, and gave them a better impression of life than after-experience verified; and catnip tea and saffron became palatable when commended by a spoon held by her. She knew the age of every one in the village, and, had politicians not rendered the word hackneyed, we would say she had the "antecedents" of every one at her fingers' ends. She was as good as an almanac for chronological dates; and in the matter of historical incidents, Dudley Leavitt and Mrs. P. generally came out neck-and-neck.

She had a great reverence for this same almanac, and we cannot refrain from speaking of an incident in connection with it. She put implicit faith in its predictions, and the weather-table stood like a guide-board to direct her on her meteorological march through the year. One year, however, everything went wrong. Storms took place that were not mentioned, and those mentioned never occurred. The moon's phases were all out of joint, and the good dame sat up all one cold night to watch for an advertised eclipse that didn't come off. For a long time she tried to vindicate her favourite, but at last, when a " windy day" predicted proved as mild a one as ever the sun shone on, her faith wavered, to be entirely overthrown by a cold north-easterly storm that had been set down for " pleasant." A timely discovery, that Ike had put a last year's almanac instead of the true one, alone saved the credit of that mathematical standard of natural law.

Her domestic virtues were of the most exalted kind. Cleanliness was with her a habit, and every windy day was sure to see Paul's regimentals upon a clothes-line, in the yard, dancing away with a levity altogether at variance with the rules of military propriety. A spider never dared to obtrude his presence upon the homestead ; a moth never corrupted the sanctuary of woollen that her care and a little camphor had touched. The white floor of the Partingtonian kitchen was as full of knots as a map of New Hampshire is of hills, from frequent scourings ; and though she never scoured through and fell into the cellar, like the Dutch damsel we read of, it did not seem at all improbable that such an event might happen.

But her benevolence was the crowning characteristic of her life, developing itself in a thousand and more ways. It sought to make every one around her happy. She commenced taking snuff with an eye solely to its social tendencies, and her box was a continual offering to friendship. When the " last war" broke out, she headed a volunteer list of patriotic women to make shirts for the soldiers, and gave them encouragement and souchong tea to work for the brave men that were exposing themselves to peril ; and she scraped Paul's only linen shirt—an heir-loom, by the way, in the family—up into lint for the wounded soldiers. A fitting spouse was she for Corporal Paul. Her reputation for benevolence was spread all over the land, like butter upon a hot Johnny-cake of her own baking, and her currant-wine for the sick got a premium for three successive years in the cattle fair.

Alas, that we have not room to pursue the theme further! We must take a flying leap over many incidents, and hasten on.

When Paul's younger brother, Peter—the Peter that went "out West," in his youth, whose wife joined the Mormons—died, he sent his little Isaac to the care of the widow of Paul, and from his earliest infancy he has been her care. She never had

any children of her own, and her solicitude is earnestly engaged
for him. He is as merry a boy as you will find any day, and,
though a little tricky and mischievous, the first beginning of
malice doesn't abide with him. His tricks do not flow from any
premeditation of fun even ; they spring spontaneously and naturally, as the lambs skip or the birds sing. Whether he takes the
bellows' nose for a cannon, or saws off the acorn on the tall, old-
fashioned chair for a top, it is all a matter of course, and his
bright face knows no cloud when rebuked for what he has done,
but he turns to new mischiefs with new zest. Such is Ike. He
is now eleven years, just upon the dividing line between account-
ability and indulgence, beyond which boyish mischief becomes
malice, to be trained by the magic of a leather strap.

Professor Wideswarth, a member of the Partington family—
like a "remarkable case" in the paper—of long standing, has
associated the two in a poem, which for sublimity is surpassed by
Coleridge's Hymn in the Valley of Chamouni : but then they are
nothing alike, and parties may divide on their respective merits.
One thing about the song, it is authentic in its details, as we have
heard averred by the old lady herself. The music, set to a
rocking-chair movement, was very popular when it was first
issued, and the editor of the *Blaze*, in a complimentary notice of
it, said no musical library could be perfect without it. The
poem we give below :—

MRS. PARTINGTON AT TEA.

Good Mistress P.
Sat sipping her tea,
Sipping it, sipping it, Isaac and she ;
What though the wind blew fiercely around,
And the rain on the pane gave a comfortless sound ;
Little cared she,
Kind Mistress P.,
As Isaac and she sat sipping their tea.

And in memory
What sights did she see,
As Isaac and she sat sipping their tea !
She turned her gaze to the opposite wall,
Where hung the portrait of Corporal Paul ;
And fancies free,
To Mistress P.,
Arose in her mind like the steam of the tea.

And little saw she,
Blind Mistress P.,
As silently she sat sipping her tea,
With her eyes on the wall and her mind away,
That Isaac was taking that time to play ;

And wicked was he
To Mistress P.,
As dreamily she sat sipping her tea.

For Isaac he,
In diablerie,
Emptied her rappee into her tea;
And the old dame tasted and tasted on,
Till she thought, good soul, that her taste was gone
For the souchong tea,
And the strong rappee,
Sorely puzzled the palate of Mistress P.

This moral, you see,
Is drawn from the tea
That Isaac had ruined for Mistress P.,
For ever will mix in the cup of our joy
The dark rappee of sorrow's alloy,
And none are free,
Any more than she,
From annoying alloys that mix with their tea.

This sketch of the life of Mrs. Partington would be imperfect, were we to omit giving a brief notice of the picture of the inestimable lady that stands as our vignette. We have long felt that an admiring public deserved a more definitive expression of her than could be gained from the mere words, however wise, that fell from her oracular lips. A sense of justice to her innumerable merits has impelled us to redeem her from the uncertainty of mere verbal delineation, and here we have produced her, the fair ideal of wise simplicity.

It was with great difficulty that we secured this boon for the world. A modest diffidence, that fifty-seven winters have not weakened, made her unwilling that her likeness should be thus submitted to the unsparing gaze of thousands. In vain we urged many illustrious examples of like martyrdom—of men who, from pure philanthropy, had sacrificed themselves in the everlasting reproach of stereotype, from the never-souring " Old Jacob" to the meek " Elder-berry," blessing the world with disinterested benevolence at a dollar a quart bottle, six bottles for five dollars. She was not to be moved by any argument we could offer, and we were about to abandon the idea in despair, when the strategy of Isaac effected what diplomacy had failed to accomplish. Snugly ensconced in an old clothes-press by Isaac for three days, our artist was enabled, through the key-hole, to watch the varied expression that flitted across her time-worn face; and his genius achieved its high triumph at the moment when Paine's gas had become the concentrated object of her thought, and, oblivious to external scene and circumstances, her mind was grappling that huge problem, in a vain effort to get a little light upon the subject.

This is the precise moment at which the artist has taken her—impaled her, so to speak, in view of its correctness, on his pencil point, and transferred her, still quick with life, to the breathing —paper.

In a short time Mrs. Partington's dear husband was no more. There were melancholy days in the Partingtonian mansion when Paul stepped out. The old chair stood by the right side of the fire-place, as if waiting to be occupied; the mug simmered in the winter evenings between the andirons with a mournful measure, as if responsive to the wind that made a muss and hurly-burly about the chimney-top; the regimentals were aired upon the clothes-line, and, inflated with wind, seemed at times like the corporal himself, cut up in parcels, who was, alas! to fill them no more. The settling of the estate broke in upon this dull and monotonous existence, and, in the excitement of the law, she forgot the sorrow that, as she said, made her nothing but flesh, skin, and bones. The remark she made concerning probate offices is recorded as a living evidence of her sagacity. Some one spoke to her about the probate proceedings regarding the estate. "Yes" said she, "it is probe it, probe it, all the time ; and if the poor, widowless body gets the whole, she don't get half enough." The remark, likewise, about doing things by attorney will be remembered until it is forgotten :—"Don't do anything by power of eternity," said she, "for, if you do, you will never see the end of it." What profundity!

On a recent occasion, while in the street with Isaac, a citizen soldier in all the pride of regulation-uniform passed them. "See!" said the boy with animation, "does that look like uncle Paul?" She looked at him half offended. "No," said she, with pride in her expression, "he is no more like your uncle than Hyperion fluid is like a satire!" There was Shakspeare and dignity in the remark, and Isaac turned with emotion to look at the picture of a monkey, in a window, tempting a chained dog by holding his tail within an inch of the canine nose.

Speaking of the monkey's tail reminds us that we are come to the end of our tale about Mrs. Partington. In the hope that he has pleased you, the biographer places his hand on his heart and bows, as the curtain descends to slow music.

MILD WEATHER.

"THIS is grand weather, mem, for poor people," said Mr
Tigh, the rich neighbour of Mrs. Partington, on a very warm
day of winter, and indulged in a half-chuckle about it as he
rubbed his hands together. It is a remark that almost everybody would make, and mean it, too,—at a time when coal, by
the rapacity of man, was 35s. or 40s. a-ton, and cold weather,
by the blessing of Heaven, that tempers the wind to the shorn
lambs and ragged children, was withheld,—but not Mrs. Partington.

"Yes," said she, gently laying her hand at the same time on
the sleeve of Mr. Tigh's coat, and looking him in the face.
"Yes, and don't folks use this good weather too much as an
excuse for not helping the indignant widows and orphanless
children? Depend upon it, cold weather is the best for the
poor, for then the rich feel the cold, and think more of 'em, and
feel more exposed to give 'em consolation and coal. Cold weather
comes down from heaven o' purpose to make men feel their duty,
and it touches the heart, as the frost touches the milk-pitcher
and breaks it, and the milk of humane kindness runs out, and
the poor are made better for it. Cold weather is a blessing to
the poor, depend upon it."

She stopped here, and Mr. Tigh cast his eyes down and struck
his cane several times against a brick at his feet; then, bidding
the old lady good morning, he moved away.

THE CHINA QUESTION.

"You never see sich chaney no ware now, as this," said Mrs.
Partington, as she took from an obscure corner of the old cupboard a teapot of antique appearance, noseless and handleless,
and cracked here and there, and stayed with putty where Time's
mischievous fingers had threatened a dissolution of the union.
"That teapot was my grandmother's afore she was married; I
remember it just as well as it was yesterday."

"Remember when your grandmother was married?" queried
Ike.

"No, no; the teapot," responded she; "and it was a perfect
beauty, with the Garden of Eden on it, and the flowers and Adam
and Eve on it, so natural that you might almost smell their
fragrance."

" What, smell Adam and Eve ?" said Ike.

" No, the flowers, stupid !" replied she; " my grand'ther gave it to her as a momento mori of his undying infection, because the colours wouldn't fade, and they never have, though children are destroying angels, and they made the mischief among the crockery, as they always do now-a-day."

She had held the teapot in her hands as she spoke, and now she gazed in silence upon the picture of Adam and Eve, partially concealed in the bushes, and she revelled in the memory of the past, and wondered if her grandmother ever came back to look at that old teapot that she had preserved so carefully, as an heir-loom ; then, carefully brushing off some dust that rested upon it, she replaced it, and charged Ike impressively to keep it most sacrilegiously for her sake. He said he would, as plain as his mouth full of preserved plums would let him, and wiped his mouth on the sleeve of his best jacket.

SYMPATHY.

" HERE'S fresh hallibut !" cried the fish-vendor, beneath Mrs. Partington's window.

" I know it is, you poor cretur !" said the estimable lady, looking after him with a commiserating expression ; " I know it is ; and I believe it is the seventh fresh *haul about* that he has made by here to-day ; and he speaks so pitiful, too, when he is telling us of it, it makes my very heart ache for him."

She caught not the *deep* significance of the cry ; but her bene-volence, always on the alert, construed it into an appeal for sympathy. Heaven's blessings on thee, Mrs. Partington, and, with reverence be it wished, where hearts are regarded, may you turn up a trump.

PAUL'S GHOST.

IT was just in the nigh edge of a summer evening, and Mrs. Partington, who had worked hard at her knitting all day, began to feel a little dozy. She felt, as she described it to her neigh-bour, Mrs. Battlegash, " a sort of alloverness ;" and those who have felt as she thus described it, will know the precise sensa-tion—for ourselves, never having felt so, we cannot explain it.

It was a sort of half twilight, when the daylight begins to be thick and muddy, and a time when ghosts are said to be round fully as plenty as at the classic hour of midnight. We never could see the propriety of restricting ghostly operations to this sombre hour, and, as far as our experience goes, we have seen as many ghosts at " noon of day" as at the "noon of night."

She never told us why, or if she were thinking of ghosts at this time ; indeed, all we know about the ghost was from Mrs. Battlegash, and we shall have to give the narration as we had it under Mrs. B.'s own hand :—

" Says Mrs. Part'nton, says she, ' Mrs. Battle,' she always calls me Battle, though my name is Battlegash—my husband's name and his father's —says she, ' Mrs. Battle, I've seen an apprehension ;' and I thought she was agoing to have an asterisk, she was so very pale and haggard like ; and says I, ' What's the matter ?" for I felt kind of skeered. I had heered a good deal about the spirituous manifestations, and didn't know but they had been a manifesting her. Says I, 'What's the matter?' agin, and then says she, as solum as a grave-yard, 'I've seen Paul!' I felt cold chills a crawlin' all over me, but I mustard courage enough to say, ' Do tell!' ' Yes,' says she, ' I saw him with my mortal eyes, just as he looked when he was a tenement of clay, with the very soger clo'es and impertinences he had on the last day he sarved his country in the auxillary.'

" I tried to comfort the poor cretur by telling her that I guessed he didn't keer enough about her to want to come back, and as his estate had all been settled sacrilegiously, it would be very unreasonable indeed in him to come back to disturb her.

" ' Where did you see him ?' says I. ' Out into the yard, said she. ' When did you see him ?' says I. ' Just now,' said she. ' Are you shore it was he?' said I, determined to get at the bottom of it. ' Yes,' said she, ' if ever an apprehension did come back, that 'ere was one. P'raps it is there now.' Then says I, ' Ruth,' says I, ' le's go and see.'

" She riz right up, and we walked along through the long entry into her room, and looked out of her back window, and there, shore enough, was a sight as froze my blood to calves-foot jelly. There was the soger cap and coat, as nateral as life, with the tompion atop. My heart come up into my mouth, so that I could have spit it out just as easy as not. Mrs. Part'nton, says she, ' What do you think of it ? isn't it his apprehension ? But I'm determined to speak to it.'

" I tried to persuade her not to, but she insisted on it, and out she went.

" ' Paul ! ' said she, ' what upon airth do you want, that you should come back arter it, so apprehensively ?' The figure was

setting on the top of the pump when she spoke, and it didn't take
no notice of her. 'Paul!' said she a little louder. Then slowly
and solemnly that 'ere cap turned round, and instead of Paul,
Mr. Editor, if you'll believe it, it was Ike, the little scapegrace,
that had frightened us almost out of our wits, if we ever had any.
That boy, I believe, will be the means of somebody's death. Mrs.
Part'nton grew very red in the face, and razed her hand to inflict
corporal punishment onto the young corporal, but the boy looked
up kind of pleasantly like, and she couldn't find the heart to
strike him, though I told her if she spared the rod she would
spile that 'ere child. It is a fortnight for him that he isn't a child
of mine, I can tell him."

Here Mrs. Battlegash's narrative ends. We can fancy the
scene in the yard: the youngster in the corporal's coat, the red
face changing to pleasant equanimity, the raised hand, indicative
of temper subsiding, as the waves do when the wind ceases to
blow, and peace, like the evening star above them, prevading and
giving grace to the tableau.

IKE SO TENDER-HEARTED.

"There, don't take on so, dear," said Mrs. Partington, as she
handed Ike a peach he had been crying for. He took the peach,
and a minute afterwards was heard whistling "Jordon" on the
ridgepole of the shed. "He is sich a tender-hearted critter,"
said she to Mrs. Sled, smilingly, while that excellent neighbour
looked at him through the window with two deprecatory eyes—
"He is so tender-hearted, that I can't ask him to go out and
draw an armful of wood, or split a pail of water, without setting
him crying at once."

She paused for Mrs. Sled's mind to comprehend the whole
force of the remark concerning Ike's lachrymosity.

"And he's the most considerate boy, too," resumed she, "that
ever you see; for when we had the inclination on the lungs, he
wouldn't take a bit of the medicine Dr. Bolus had subscribed,
'cause he knowed it would do me good, and said he'd full as lieves
take molasses!"

She went on with her knitting, and Ike became lost in the
foot of a stocking that she was toeing out. Those grapes on the
trellis opposite where Ike is sitting look tempting!

Mrs. Partington says there must be some sort of kin between
poets and pullets, for they both are always chanting their lays.

LOOK UP.

PERHAPS it would not make a rap's difference, one way or the other, in a man's fortunes, whether he looked up or down; but we always fancied that there was a reason for the superstition that made a man's habit of looking down an augury of his success in life; as if his mind, dwelling, with his eyes, continually on the earth, would better enable him to know how to make money, as a man who dwells in the darkness can see better in the accustomed obscurity than one who comes directly in from the light. He keeps his eyes on the ground, and no stray fourpences or pence escape his eagle vision. Every rag is marked to see if it may not be a bill in disguise, and the hope to find a pocket-book or two, while passing along the street, seems to be continually present in his mind. His eyes grow heavy with looking down, and when at last there is no longer occasion to look down,—when he has found all the fourpences and pocket-books that he has sought for,—then the light is painful to him, and he turns to the earth again, before he is dead. Habit makes it his only happiness, and he goes to seeking for pocket-books and fourpences again.

If this be the result of looking down, the result of looking up must be, we should suppose, the opposite of this. Lifting the eyes above the world brings one to view things far better than fourpences. As much difference between them as the difference between a star of the first magnitude and a gold sovereign. The eyelids turned up, the sunlight streams down upon the mind, and prepares therein a soil for the reception of good seed, that shall grow up and bear fruit.

Look up! Who ever thinks of groping about the foundations of the National Monument, when there are so many pleasures of vision to be gained by climbing to its summit? The higher the look, or climb, the broader the view from the lofty position one gains. The most beautiful and delicate work of a structure is placed at the top. The fruit that is sweetest is always the nearest the sun. These are facts that belong to every-day life, to say nothing of that spiritual looking-up required to give light to the soul; a commodity which some few people possess, and seem desirous of benefiting.

But don't, in looking up, lose all memory of earth; for you can't drop your body as you can your coat, with your wish, and soar off on the wings of the spirit. When you look up, keep part of an eye directed to the earth, and avoid the coal-holes and cellar-ays that are open for your unwary feet. A too deep absorption in things above the earth, may make the star gazer conscious of a pain in the back, from a too sudden contact with the "cold, cold ground," as we saw a printer served on a cold morning (though whether he was heaven-seeking is questionable), and who looked very simple as he gathered himself up after the prostration.

Let the upward look characterise us all,—with an eye to accidents mentioned above,—and secure for us a name for aspiring above the grovelling things of the world, and five of us out of six may be deserving of it. Look up!

A SOLEMN FACT.

"Your plants are most flagrantly odious," said Mrs. Partington, as she stooped over a small oval red table in a neighbour's house, which table was covered with cracked pots filled with luxuriant geraniums, and a monthly rose, and a cactus, and other bright creations, that shed their sweetness upon the almost tropical atmosphere of a southerly room in April, while a fragrant vine, hung in chains, graced the window with a curtain more gorgeous than any other not exactly like it. Mrs. Partington stood gazing upon them in admiration.

"How beautiful they are!" she continued. "Do you profligate your plants by slips, mem?"

She was told that such was the case; they were propagated by slips.

"So was mine," said Mrs. P. "I was always more lucky with my slips than with anything else."

Bless thy kind old heart, Mrs. Partington! it may be so with you, but it is not so with all; for the way of the world is hard, and many slips are made, and for the unfortunates whose feet or tongues slip on the treacherous path, a sentence generally awaits which admits small chance of reversal,—a soiled coat or a soiled character sticking to them until both are worn out. Dear old lady! your humble chronicler remembers that many of the young and beautiful are *profligated* by slips,—slips so gradual that propriety could hardly call them such at first—which end, heaven and earth and predition know how deep.

NEW REMEDY FOR A DROUGHT.

MRS. PARTINGTON was in the country one August, and for a whole month not one drop of rain had fallen. One day she was slowly walking along the road, with her umbrella over her head, when an old man, who was mending up a little gap of wall, accosted her, at the same time depositing a large stone on the top of the pile.

"Mrs. Partington, what do *you* think can help this 'ere drought?"

The old lady looked at him through her spectacles, at the same time smelling a fern leaf.

"I think," said she, in a tone of oracular wisdom, "I think a little rain would help it as much as anything."

It was a great thought. The old gentleman took off his straw hat, and wiped his head with his cotton handkerchief, at the same time saying that he thought so too.

"HEAR THAT VOICE."

DID the reader ever know a man grown, and big at that, with a very small voice, that almost squealed in uttering itself, and gave a most ridiculous aspect to what was perhaps of great importance, as matters of life and death, the reading of a will, an exhortation to virtue, or an anxious inquiry concerning the health of friends? Of course he has, for there are many such voices about. An agent of a large manufacturing establishment in Yorkshire possessed this peculiarity of voice to a remarkable degree, which once was the cause of a most mortifying and ludicrous mistake. A man came to the factory to get employment, a great burly fellow with a voice like young thunder, and saluted the agent—who was a small man, by the way—with the question, "Do you want to hire?" in a tone that seemed to shake the room in which they stood. Starting at the sound, and with a face expressive of nervous irritability, he drawled out, in his squeaking, querulous manner, as if looking at each word before he uttered it,

"No—I—don't—know—as—I—do."

The man, not understanding his peculiarity, attributed the strange tones to another cause, and, kindly extending his huge hand, as one might suppose a friendly bear would, under like circumstances, patted the little agent on the head, and soothingly uttered—

"Well, well, my little fellow, don't *cry about it;* don't take on so, if you can't hire me!"

The contact of crude humanity with his delicate head operated as magically upon the agent as did the touch of Captain Cuttle's hook upon the refined flesh of Dombey, and frightful was the yell with which he met the mechanic's sympathy in a command to leave the room, and awfully vehement was the manner in which he slammed the door to as the good-humoured fellow passed into the street.

MRS. PARTINGTON PENNED.

A FRIEND, returning from a visit to New York, presented to Mrs. Partington a gold pen which had been entrusted to him for her. The present was duly examined and admired, and turned round, and pulled out, and held up to the light, and a receipt for pew-rent was brought out from the black bureau, on the back of which to test its quality, and she made a straight mark to the right, and then crossed it with another straight mark of equal length, and then said it was charming.

"But who are they?" said she, speculatively. "I don't know them, I'm shore."

The friend blandly explained that they knew her very well, and that this present was a tribute of regard for her many virtues, which, like the odour of ten thousand flowers, is borne across the entire land. The giver was eloquent, touching.

"Ah," said she, "it is very kind to remember a poor widow-less body like me! What friends I have got! I hope that Heaven will be rewarded for their kindness to me!"

It was a fervent aspiration, and though the letter of her prayer might seem to divert the reward from its true object, still its spirit conferred it rightly. She opened the old black bureau-desk in the corner, and placed the gold pen carefully by the side of the paste shoe-buckles, and hoop earrings—valuable relics of by-gone times—and then securely locked the desk, as she saw Ike looking curiously into the window, with his nose flattened close against the glass.

THE SODA FOUNTAIN.

"THERE it goes again!" said Mrs. Partington, as she became conscious of the sublimity of a soda fountain one warm day. "There it goes again, I declare, fizzin away like a blessed old

C

locomoco on the railroad. Don't say anything about Nigary now
—that is n't nothin in comparison to this—and it a'n't *bad* beer
nuthur; but how in natur they can draw so many kinds out of one
fassit, that's the wonderment to me!" and she re-adjusted her
specs, and took a new survey of the mystery, while Ike, unwatched,
was weighing his knife and five jackstones in the bright brass
scale on the other counter.

GIVING REASONS.

THE various reasons which some folks always have ready for
their accidents and misfortunes, or as palliatives for their faults
and follies, are very amusing. Many stories are told of such.
One we remember of a boy who had played truant, and gave as
the reason for his absence that his father kept him at home to
help to grind the handsaw. A toper, accounting for a bad cold
he had, said he had slept on the common, and forgot to shut the
gate. Another soaker, who was found in the gutter, with the
water making a free passage over him, when asked how he came
there, replied that he had agreed to meet a man there.

In our printing-office days, when we had to work for a living,
it was our luck to work with a queer old fellow, who bore the
name of Smith, or some such odd title. He was a very unhappy
man, and never smiled unless he had the whole office in a snarl,
and then he would chuckle right gladly. He was always fancying
that his office-mates were imposing upon him, and a perfect flood
of bile would he throw off at times for imagined wrongs. His
position was by a window, fronting the east, and over this window
he claimed absolute dominion, to shut it up or have it open, as he
just pleased, maugre the fretting of those who were annoyed by
his obstinacy. He assumed the office of a thermometer for the
men, and graduated the heat according to his own feelings. If
the wind was east, he would as surely have the window open as
that he would have it shut if it blew pleasantly from the west.

One day, with the wind blue east, the window was open all
day, and much audible complaint was made by all hands, but
without any effect. It was with a feeling nearly akin to exulta-
tion they saw him enter the office next day with indubitable signs
of having a cold upon him; his nose looked " red and raw," and
his voice sounded as if he had two tight-fitting cork stoppers in
his nostrils. The window that day was not opened, you may
depend. One of the men undertook to remind him that his cold
was in consequence of the wind blowing upon him.

" Do it aidt," said Smith, " but I hug by hat up by the widnder, ad last dight whed I put it od, it was brib full of east wid."

A SMALL TRADE.

" COLD day, Mr. Smith," said old Roger, in the Dock Square omnibus to his neighbour, who assented very politely. "And yet," continued Roger, " cold as it is, I have just seen a man in State Street, who does not wear gloves."

" Ah!" responded Smith, struck with the singularity of the statement, " why not, pray?"

" Why," chuckled the old man, "because he has n't any hands."

Mr. Smith smiled.

ON LOCOMOTION.

" So they 've got you on the stage, Mrs. Partington," said we to the old lady, after seeing her name on a theatre bill, as one of the characters in a new burletta.

" On the stage!" replied she, and a gleam of memory passed over her face like a ray of sunshine over a faded landscape, and as she looked out of the window, and down the street, until her eye rested on an omnibus moving quickly along, in the pride of paint and gold, and she took passage in it, in fancy, and went along with it. " Yes," said she, " they did get me on the stage, because it caused a nonsense in my stomach to ride inside; and what a queer figure I did make on it, to be sure! But that, dear, was five and twenty years ago, and it is so queer they should remember it. O, them stages! I 've heerd of people riding by easy stages, but I never saw one. The easiest way that I ever rid was on a pillory behind Paul, there. Easy stages, indeed! why, it shook me as if it would shake the census all out of me, and I never got over it for a week. How different it is now!"—and she looked at the omnibus just passing her door, —" all you 've to do is to get into an ominous, all cushioned nicely, with a whole picture-gallery round it, to see for nothing, and afore you know it you are where you want to go. Stages ―"

" But it is the National stage," we said.

" Well, well," replied she, hastily, " 'taint no difference; only the National stage carried the mail, and t'other the female passengers; one was jest as bad as t'other, and I don't know but worse."

"But they 've got you in the theatre, the National Theatre," we persisted, and showed her the bill.

She looked at it a moment, and wiped her specs, and looked at it again in silence, as if her mind had n't got back from the hard journey it had just taken. At that moment a crash of glass called her hastily to the kitchen. The floor was covered with fragments of that brittle article, and a large ball hopped under a chair, as if ashamed of itself; while Ike was seen, through the broken window, making tracks speedily for the shed. We left her picking up the glass, so that he might not get it into his bare feet when he came in. Depend upon it, he had to take a severe "talking to" when she caught him.

THE LARGEST LIBERTY.

"Now go to meeting, dear," said Mrs. Partington, as Isaac stood smoothing his hair, preparatory to going out on Sunday. He looked down at his new shoes, and a thought of the green fields made him sigh. A fishing-line hung out of one pocket, which Mrs Partington did n't see.

"Where shall I go to?" asked Ike.

Since the old lady had given up her seat in the Old North church, she had no stated place of worship.

"Go," replied she sublimely, as she pulled down his jacket behind, "go anywheres where the Gospel is dispensed with."

Such liberality is rare. Bigotry finds no place in her composition, and the truth, in her view, throws its light into every apartment of the Christian edifice, like an oysterman's chandelier into his many booths. The simile is not the very best, but the best to be had at present.

MRS. PARTINGTON IN COURT.

"I took my knitting-work and went up into the gallery," said Mrs. Partington, the day after visiting one of the city courts; "I went up into the gallery, and, after I had digested my specs, I looked down into the room, but I could n't see any courting going on. An old gentleman seemed to be asking a good many impertinent questions,—just like some old folks,—and people were sitting round making minuets of the conversation. I don't see how they made out what was said, for they all told different stories. How much easier it would be to get along if they were all made to tell the same story! What a sight of trouble it would save the lawyers! The case, as they call it, was given to the jury, but I couldn't see it, and a gentleman with a long pole was made to swear that he'd keep an eye on 'em, and see that they didn't run away with it. Bimeby in they come agin, and then they said somebody was guilty of something, who had just said he was innocent, and didn't know nothing about it no more than the little baby that never had subsistence. I come away soon afterwards; but I couldn't help thinking how trying it must be to sit there all day, shut out from the blessed air!"

This experience is a beautiful exhibit of judicial life. True enough, Mrs. Partington; how easy might be the determining of cases, were but one side of the story told! But, alas for perplexed jurymen! there are unfortunately two sides, and the brain is racked to judge between them—Conscience holding the light tremblingly, lest Honour be compromised, and Mercy pointing with raised finger to its fountain, as if endeavouring to draw attention from Justice, who stands, sword in hand, to urge her claim. " To well and truly try" is the solemn duty fastened by an oath, and the country reposes in blessed security upon the broad responsibility of twelve honest men.

"RIGHT" AND "LEFT."

"THERE never was a time when the divine *right* of kings could be better shown," said old Roger, emphasizing the word " right" significantly.

" Why?" asked the little man from the provinces, looking up.

" Because," replied he, " there will soon be none of them *left.*"

An audible " *Whew!*" whistled along the table, and one distinct knock from each boarder, denoted equivocal approbation. The dessert was dispensed with.

A LITTLE TRUTH WELL PUT.

" So you've come down to attend the adversary meetings," said Mrs. Partington, as she surveyed the three trunks and two valises and a basket that the cab had just left, and the owner of them all, a gentleman in black, with a ghostly-looking neckcloth.

" Ah " said he, humouring her conceit and smiling, for he
expected to stay some days, " the adversary we meet we subdue
with the weapons of the Spirit."

" That is just what dear Deacon Sprig said when he captivated
the crazy Ingen with British Jamaica rum, and then put him in
bride'll. Says he, ' I'll subdue him with the sword of the spirit'
—he was such a queer man ! These meetings are excellent for
converting heathens and saving the lost, and I do hope, after they
have saved everybody else, that they will try and save a few more
of their own that need teaching. There is a great many round
here that want looking after more than the heathen do ; and we
must look after our own first, or be worse than the infiddles."

A pair of yarn stockings and a box of butter stopped her mouth
for the time, and the old silver spoons marked " P. P." and the
antique china were brought out—articles that were only used on
state occasions.

MUSICAL CRITICISM.

" How did you like the concert, " asked Frank, of Mrs. Partington, " at the Oratorio ?"   " Very much, indeed," said she ; " I
liked everything about the Ontario but the consecutives ; the
corrosives I thought was sublimated, but the consecutives I
thought was dreadfully out of tune." Frank explained to her
the object of the recitative, and smiled a little at the queer
mistake she had made in musical terms. Bless thee, Mrs.
Partington ! thy genius in its extravagance is never retarded by
terms.

FANCY DISEASES.

" Diseases is very various," said Mrs. Partington, as she returned from a street-door conversation with Dr. Bolus. " The
Doctor tells me that poor old Mrs. Haze has got two buckles on
her lungs ! It is dreadful to think of, I declare. The diseases
is so various ! One way we hear of people's dying of hermitage
of the lungs ; another way of the brown creatures ; here they tell
us of the elementary canal being out of order, and there about
tonsors of the throat ; here we hear of neurology in the head,
there of an embargo ; one side of us we hear of men being killed
by getting a pound of tough beef in the sarcofagus, and there
another kills himself by discovering his jocular vein. Things

change so, that I declare I don't know how to subscribe for any
disease now-a-days. New names and new nostrils takes the
place of the old, and I might as well throw my old herb-bag
away."

Fifteen minutes afterwards, Isaac had that herb-bag for a tar-
get, and broke three squares of glass in the cellar window in
trying to hit it, before the old lady knew what he was about. She
didn't mean exactly what she said.

DAGUERREOTYPES.

"What artfulness!" said Mrs. Partington, as she held her
miniature in her hand, done in the highest style of the Daguerrean
art. The features were radiant with benevolence; the cap, close-
fitted about her venerable face, bore upon it the faded black rib-
bon, the memento of ancient woe; the close-folded kerchief about
her neck was pinned with mathematical exactness, while from
beneath the cap border struggled a dark-gray lock of hair, like a
withered branch in winter, waving amid accumulated snows. The
specs and box were represented upon the table by her side. The
picture was like her, and admiration marked every line of her
countenance as she spoke.

"What artfulness here is, and how nat'rally every liniment is
brought out! How nicely the dress is digested!"

She was talking to herself all the while.

"Why, this old black lutestring, that I have worn twenty year
for Paul, looks as good as new, only it is a little too short-waisted
by a great deal. O, Paul, Paul!" sighed she, as she sat back in
her chair, and gazed, with a tear in her eye, upon an old smoke-
stained profile, cut in black, that had hung for many a year above
the mantel-piece. "O, Paul! what a blessed thing this is, where
Art helps Natur, and Natur helps Art, and they both help one
another! How I wish I had your dear old phismahogany done
like this! I'd prize it more than gold or silver."

She sat still, and looked alternately at the Daguerreotype and
the profile, as if she hoped the profile would speak to her; but it
still looked rigidly forward, thrusting out its huge outline of nose as
if proud of it, and then with a sigh she reclasped the case, and
deposited the picture in the upper drawer of the old black bureau
in the corner. Ike was all the while burning holes through
a pine shingle with one of Mrs. Partington's best knitting
needles.

THAT AND THAT.

"You do make that child look like a fool, wife, with all that toggery on him," said Mr. Fog, angrily, as they were starting out for a walk. "Dear me," says Mrs. Partington, meeting them at the door, "what a doll of a baby, and how much he resembles his papa!" Mr. Fog coughed, and they passed along.

ON POLITICS.

"As regards these electrical matters," said Mrs. Partington, just before election—she lived on a main street, and the cheering and noise of parties passing her door kept her awake o' nights—"I don't see the use of making so much fuss about it. Why don't they take some one and give him their sufferings, if he has n't got any of his own, and let him be governor till he dies, just as they do the judges, and arterwards too, as they sometimes do them, for they might as well be dead, a good many of 'em? O, this confusion of noise and hubbub! My poor head aches o' hearing of it, and Isaac has got sich a cold, looking out of the window at the possessions without nothing on the head. And then what critters they all be, to be sure!—their newspapers are brim full of good desolations, but ne'eraone of 'em did I ever know 'em to keep. They are always resolving, like the showman's resolving views, and one resolution fades away jest as quick as another comes. If I could have my way, I would"—

"Hooray! here they come!" cried Ike, breaking in upon the old lady's remarks, and banging his slate on the floor, and throwing up the window with a vehemence that broke two squares of glass.

"Hooray!" came up in a big chorus from the street, filling Mrs. Partington's little chamber, to its utmost capacity, with "hooray," the great element of political life.

"There they go agin," cried she, "with their drums and lanterns, like crazy critters, and keeping folks awake when they ought to be in the arms of Murphy!"

Ike pulled in his head and dropped the window, and the good old lady mended the fracture of the glass by a hat and a pair of pants of Ike's, with the threat of severe punishment if he ever did so again. But do you suppose she would have kept it? Ike knew better. When the glazier came in the next day to mend the window, she had to tell him the story of how it was broke, but all the blame was on the politicians.

BEAUTIFUL REFLECTION INTERRUPTED.

"DEAR me!" said Mrs. Partington; and so she *is* dear—not
that she meant so—because under that black bonnet is humility,
and self-praise forms no part of her reflection. It was a simple
ejaculation, that was all; our word for it. "Dear me! here they
are going to have war again over the sea, and only for a Turkey,
and it don't say how much it weighed either, nor whether it was
tender; and Prince Knockemstiff has gone off in a miff, and the
Ruslin bears and Austriches are all to be let loose to devour the
people, and Heaven knows where the end of it will leave off.
War is a dreadful thing, so destroying to temper and good clo'es,
and men shoot at each other jest as if they was gutter purchase,
and cheap at that."

How sorrowfully the cover of the snuff-box shut, as she ceased
speaking! and the spectacles looked dewy, like a tumbler in
summer-heat filled with ice-water, as she looked at the profile of
the corporal, with the sprig of sweet fern above it, and the old
sword behind the door.

What did Ike mean as he stole in, and deposited some red
article under the cricket upon which her feet rested, and then
stole out again?

A hissing sound followed—crack! snap! bang! whiz! went a
bunch of crackers—and Mrs. Partington, in consternation and
cloth slippers, danced about the room, forgetful of distant war in
her present alarm.

Ah, Ike!

APPOINTING INSPECTORS.

"INSPECTORS of customs!" said Mrs. Partington, energetically,
as she laid down the paper chronicling some new appointment.
Here was a new idea, that broke upon her mind like a ray of
sunshine through a corn barn.

"Inspectors of customs!" and she looked up at the rigid profile of the old corporal, as if she would ask what he had to say
about it; but that warrior had hung there too long to be now disturbed by trifles, and he took no notice of her.

"Inspectors of customs!" continued she, as she turned her
attention to the old black teapot, and then turned out the tea,
which celestial beverage gurgled through the spout, in harmony
with her reflections, not too strong; "that's a new idea to me.

But, thank Providence, I ha'n't got no customs that I had n't as lives they'd inspect as not; only I'd a little rather they wouldn't. I wish everybody could say so, but I'm afeard there are many customs that won't bear looking into. Well, let every tub stand on its own bottom, I say—I won't cast no speciousness on nobody. But I don't see what they wanted to appoint any more for, and be to so much suspense when every place has so many in it that will inspect customs for nothing. If they'd only make my next-door neighbour, Miss Juniper, now, an inspector of customs, they would n't need another for a long ways, that's mortally sartin."

She stirred her souchong as she ruminated, untasting; and Ike helped himself, unheeded, to the last preserved pear there was in the dish.

MRS. PARTINGTON AT TEA.

"ADULTERATED tea!" said Mrs. Partington, as she read in the *Transcript* an account of the adulteration of teas in England, at which she was much shocked. "I wonder if this is adulterated?" and she bowed her head over the steaming and fragrant decoction in the cup before her, whose genial odours mingled with the silvery vapour, and encircled her venerable poll like a halo. "It smells virtuous," continued she, smiling with satisfaction, "and I know this Shoo-shon tea must be good, because I bought it of Mr. Shoo-shon himself, at Redding's. Adulterated!" she meandered on, pensively as a brook in June, "and it's agin the commandment, too, which says——don't break that, Isaac!" as she saw that interesting juvenile amusing himself with making refracted sunbeams dance upon the wall, and around the dark profile, and among the leaves of the sweet fern, like yellow butterflies or fugitive chips of new June butter. The alarm for her crockery dispelled all disquietude about the tea, and she sipped her beverage, all oblivious of dele-tea-rious infusions.

SIR, YOU OWE ME A CENT.

"OTHER things may be great," said old Roger with a nod, "besides what's called so; some very *little* thing, if 'tis done well, can be a great one; in impudence, say, for instance. Yesterday a boy asked me pitifully for a fourpence; I gave him what I thought to be one, and passed on. Presently I felt a twitch at my coat-tail, and looked round, and there stood the boy. 'Sir,' says he, 'you *owe me a cent*; this 'ere won't pass for but five cents, it's crossed!' I gave the little rascal a shilling at once; I could n't help it. The thing was sublime, admirable; hang me if it was n't." And the little man struck his cane violently on the ground, and laughed happily at the supreme impudence displayed in the affair.

GUESSING AT A NAME.

"DRIVE him out!" screamed Mrs. Partington, as Ike whistled in an immense house-dog, who perambulated the kitchen, dotting the newly-washed floor with flowers of mud, and audaciously smelling Mrs. Partington's toes, as the old lady stood up in a chair to avoid him.

"Drive him out. What is his name, Isaac?"

"Guess," replied Ike.

"I can't, I know. Perhaps it's Watch, or Ponto, or Cæsar— what is it?'

"Why, Guess."

"I tell you I can't guess. Perhaps it's Hector, or Tiger, or Rover—what is his name?"

"Guess."

"O, you provoking creatur! I'll be tempered to whip you within an inch of your skin if you provoke me so. Why don't you tell me?"

"I did tell you the first time," whined Ike, pulling the dog's ear with one hand while he wiped his dry eyes with the other, "his name is Guess."

The old lady was melted by his emotion; and, as soon as the dog was sent out, some nice quince jelly settled the difficulty.

"He is such a queer child!" murmured she; "so bright! I suppose 'twas because he was weaned on pickles."

Ike ate his preserves in silence, but his eye was on the acorn on the post of the old lady's high-backed chair, and he thought what a nice top it would make if he could saw it off some day.

BURNING WATER.

"WELL, this is a discovery!" exclaimed Mrs. Partington smilingly, as she stood with a small picture in her right hand, her left resting upon the pine table, and her eyes fixed upon the flame of a glass lamp, that sputtered for a moment and then shot out a gleam of cheerful light that irradiated every part of the little kitchen, revealing the portrait of Paul upon the wall and Ike asleep by the fire. She spoke to herself—it was a way she had—and she met with no contradiction from that quarter. "This is a discovery. This lamp was almost burnt out, and I've filled it up with water, and it burns like the real ile." The experiment was perfectly triumphant; the problem of light from water was demonstrated; and yet, with this vast fact revealed to her, Mrs. Partington, with a modesty equal to that of the great philosopher who picked up a pocketful of rocks on the shore of the vast ocean of Truth, smiled with delight at her discovery, nor once thought of putting out a patent or selling rights—was entirely willing all might burn water that could.

A STRIKING MANIFESTATION.

"I can't believe in sperituous knockings," said Mrs. Partington, solemnly, as some things were related to her which had been seen, that appeared very mysterious. "I can't believe about it; for I know, if Paul could come back, he would revulge himself to me here, and wouldn't make me run a mile only to get a few dry knocks. Strange that the world should be so superstitional as to believe sich a rapsody, or think a sperrit can go knocking about like a boy in vexation. I can't believe it, and I don't know's I could if that teapot there was to jump off the table right afore my eyes!" She paused, and through the gloom of approaching darkness could be seen the determined expression of her mouth. A slight movement was heard upon the table, and the little black teapot moved from its position, crawled slowly up the wall, and then hung passively by the side of the profile of the ancient corporal! The old lady could not speak, but held up her hands in wild amazement, while her snuff-box fell from her nerveless grasp, and rolled along upon the sanded floor. She left the room to procure a light, and, as soon as she had gone, the teapot was lowered by the invisible hand to its original station, and Ike stepped out from beneath the table, stowing a long string away in his pocket, and grinning prodigiously.

IKE AND THE ELEPHANT.

"Well," said Ike, looking the elephant directly in the eye, at the same time doubling up his huge fist, as big as a penny roll, and putting on an air of defiance, after the animal had stolen his gingerbread; "well, you got it, didn't you, you old thief, you! I s'pose you think you've done thunderin' great things, don't you? For my part, I don't call it no better 'n stealing. O, you may stand there and swing that ridic'lous looking trunk o' your'n just as much as you're a mind to; you can't skeer a fellow, I tell you! This is a free country, old club-feet; and you an't agoing to take any more liberties here like that. I can tell you it won't be safe for that Ingee-rubber hide o' your'n, if you do! You take my gingerbread away agin', if you dare, that's all! You just try it, you ongainly reptile, you! O, you may look saucy, and pretend you don't keer, but you just say two words—just knock that chip off my head—and if I don't give you fits, my name an't Ike Partington, that's all! Just put down that big Ingee-rubber bludgeon, and I'll black your eyes for you, you old tough-leather! You darsn't say a word, you ill-mannered old hunch! I'd knock your eye-teeth out, if you did. O, take it up, if you're a mind to; you needn't think to bully it over me, because you're a little bigger'n I am, I can tell you. We don't stand no such nonsense as that, round here. If 't warn't for that p'leceman looking here, I'd pitch into you like a thousand o' bricks. I wouldn't get out o' your way as people do when you come along, and I should like to see you just step on my toes—why can't you just try it now, will you? I guess I'd make you hear thunder with them leather-apron ears o' your'n, you big overgrown vagabond, you! 'T a'n't no use o' talking to you, but I shall be here; and, if you don't mind your eye, I'll lick you like blazes afore I go out."

Here Isaac undoubled his hands, and, shaking his head threateningly at the huge animal, he went over to get a look at the monkeys; while the elephant lazily swung his trunk from side to side, and good-naturedly fanned himself with his big ears, as if he hadn't minded a word the little fellow had said.

WHOLESOME ADVICE

"ISAAC," said Mrs. Partington, as that interesting juvenile was playing a game of "knuckle up" against the kitchen wall, to the imminent danger of the old clock which ticked near by, "this is a marvellous age, as Deacon Babson says, and perhaps there's no harm in 'em; but I'm afeard no good 'll come out of it—no good at all—for you to keep playing marvels all the time, as you do, I am afeard you will learn how to gambol, and become a

bad boy, and forget all the good device I have given you. Ah!
it would break my soul, Isaac, to have you given to naughty
tricks, like some wicked boys that I know, who will be rake-
shames in the airth if they don't die before their time comes. So
don't gambol, dear, and always play as if you had just as lieves
the minister would see you as not." She handed him a little
bag she had made for him to keep his marbles in, and patted his
head kindly as he went again to play. Ike was fortified, for the
next five minutes, against temptation to do evil; but

> " Chase span, in the ring,
>   Knuckle up, or anything,"

are potent when arrayed against out-of-sight solicitude, and we
fear that the boy forgot. There is much reason in the old lady's
fear.

A GHOST STORY.

In the vicinity of a town not many miles from Boston, was a
dark glen, by the roadside, reputed to be haunted. A traveller
had been found here, many years before, frozen to death, and his
troubled spirit, with a disposition to trouble everybody else, was
said nightly to visit the scene of his mortal termination, to have
a "melancholy satisfaction" all alone by himself, or with but
such auditors as he could press in to participate in the "services
of the evening." An old fellow, who resided in the town, and
was fully imbued with the superstition, had been one night to a
husking, where the milk-punch had circulated with more than
common generosity, and though "na fou," he had enough on
board to make him comfortable and happy, and

> ——— " glorious,
>   O'er all the ills of life victorious."

Towards the hour of breaking up, the conversation turned upon
the ghost, by whose dark hunting-ground our friend had to pass,
over a road raised up amid an alder swamp, whose sad gloom
could hardly be dispelled by a noon-day sun, and where nothing
but a ghost of the most simple sort would wish to abide.

> " Wi' tippenny we fear nae evil,
>   Wi' usquebe we'll face the devil,"

Burns said; and milk-punch we suppose to be about the same in
its courage-inspiring properties. Our hero snapped his fingers

at danger from ghosts and unholy angels, and cared for neither a "bodle." It was a mile-walk, good, to the spiritual precinct, and, thinking on his way that it would be the part of prudence to prepare for emergency, before he came to the dark gulf he was to pass, he gathered a small artillery from a stone wall, determined, if assaulted, to do battle manfully, for the credit of the punch.

He had crossed a little brook that murmured beneath the rude bridge above it, and had fairly got through the dangerous part, as he considered it, of his journey, and muttered to himself, in rather a tone of disappointment, "I guess he must be sick; fog isn't good for him," when, lo! almost directly in the path before him was an object that made him come to a stand at once. It was all ghostly white, and he had barely time to look at it, when a hideous groan came towards him on the night air, which the milk-punch could hardly counteract in its effect on his nervous system. Rallying, however, he selected a missile, and let fly at his ghostly obstructor; another groan, like the last bellow of expiring nature, answered this assault. He hurled another huge stone, and, gathering courage from the excitement, he blazed away in a manner that would astonish either human or superhuman antagonists; but without any apparent effect upon the adversary, who stood his ground manfully, or, perhaps, we should say ghostfully. As the last stone of his ammunition was expended, however, with a cry that echoed fearfully through the alders, the ghost rushed towards him, and a violent shock laid him senseless upon the ground, a vanquished man. He was found the next morning pensively sitting by the road-side, contemplating the scene of his night's exploit, with his head in his hand.

He told his story, and pointed to the scattered missiles for proof of what he had done; and he was believed, for "to give up the ghost" was out of the question. But, in going home, a small white two-year-old bull was seen grazing by the roadside, and suspicion for a moment crossed their minds that this might have been the ghost, after all, seen through the medium of the punch; but this would have been voted rank heresy against the ancient institution of ghosts, and they held their peace.

A DANGEROUS POSITION.

"Don't lay in that postur, dear," said Mrs. Partington to Ike, who was stretched upon a settle, with his heels a foot or two higher than his head. "Don't lay so; raise yourself up, and put this pillow under you. I knew a young man once who had a suggestion of the brain in consequence of laying so—his brains all run down into his head!" and with this admonition she left him, to practise, soon after, the hazardous experiment of tying his legs in a bow knot round his neck, as he had seen Professor Baldwin do.

A LESSON ON SYMPATHY.

"WHAT a to-do they are making about this Cosset!" said Mrs. Partington smilingly. The news had reached her ears of the triumphs of Kossuth, and the name had assumed a form, and that form recalled a train of peculiar and characteristic associations, and she went on like an eight-day clock: "A cosset is a pretty thing in a family where there is children, and they are dear critters for girls that hasn't got sweethearts to invent their young affectations on; but what's the use of making such a fuss about it?"

"But this is Kos-*suth*, aunt, the great Hungarian," said Ike, tremendously, who was well posted up in passing matters; "who has come over here to ask our sympathy, and enlist us in behalf of his country."

"Well," said she, as the new light dawned upon her, "they may have our sympathy in welcome, 'cause it don't cost anything; but we musn't 'list and give 'em money,—that would be agin our constitutions!"

And the prudent dame drummed thoughtfully on her snuff-box cover, with her eyes fixed upon the vane of the Old South, while Ike amused himself by scratching "KOSSUTH," with a fork, on the end of the new japanned waiter.

HOW IKE DROPPED THE CAT.

"Now, Isaac," said Mrs. Partington, as she came into the room with a basket snugly covered over, "take our Tabby, and drop her somewhere, and see that she don't come back again, for I am sick and tired of driving her out of the butter. She is the thievinest creatur! But don't hurt her, Isaac; only take care that she don't come back."

Ike smiled as he received his charge, and the old lady felt happy in getting rid of her trouble without resorting to violence. See would rather have endured the evil of the cat, great as that evil was, than that the poor quadruped should be inhumanly dealt

with. She saw Ike depart, in the dusk of the evening, and
watched him until he became lost to view in the shadow of a tree.
It was a full half hour before he returned with his empty basket,
and an unusual glee marked his appearance; it sparkled in his
eye, it glowed in his cheek, it sported in his hair; and Ike looked
really handsome as he stood before the dame, and proclaimed the
success of his mission.

"Did she drop easy, Isaac?" asked the old lady, looking upon
him kindly, "and won't she come back?"

"She dropt just as easy!" said Ike, letting his basket fall on
the floor, and shying his cap upon the table, somewhat endangering a glass lamp with a wooden bottom that stood thereon; "she
dropt just as easy! and she won't come back; you may bet high
on that."

"But you didn't beat and mangle her, Isaac, did you? If you
did, I should be afraid she would come back and haunt us—I
have heard of such things;" and she looked anxiously in his face;
but, detecting there no trace of guilt, she patted him on the head,
and parted his hair, and told him to sit down and eat his supper,
which the young gentleman did with considerable unction.

"Isaac! Isaac!" screamed Mrs. Partington, at the foot of the
little stairway that led to the attic where the boy slept, the next
morning after the above occurrence. "Isaac!"—and he came
down stairs slowly, rubbing his eyes as he came. She had disturbed his morning nap.

"Isaac," said she, "what is that hanging yonder to a limb of
our apple-tree?" One scattering tree, as she said, constituted
her whole orchard, unless she counted the poplar by the corner.

"I can't see so fur off," said Ike, still rubbing his eyes.

"Well, I should think it was a cat; and it looks to me like our
Tabby. O, Isaac! if you have done this?" and a tone akin to
horror trembled in her voice.

"I'll go and see if it's her," said Ike, as if not hearing the last
part part of her remark; and he dashed out of the door, but soon
came back, with wonder depicted on every feature of his expressive countenance. "O, it's her! sure enough, it's her!" cried
he, "but I did drop her!"

"Well, how could she come there, then?" and the good old
lady looked puzzled.

"I'll tell you how I guess it was," said Ike, looking demurely
up. "I guess that she committed suicide, because we was going
to drop her; they are dreadful knowing critters, you know."

"True enough," replied the old lady, while something like a
tear glistened in her eye—her pity was excited; "true enough,

D

Isaac, and I dare say she thought hard of us for doing it; but she hadn't ought to, if she'd have considered a minute."

Ike said no more, but went out and cut down the supposed suicide, with a serious manner, and buried her beneath her gallows, deep down among the roots of the old tree, and she never came back.

The old lady told the story to the minister, and Ike vouched for it, but the good man shook his head incredulously at the idea of the suicide, and looked at the boy. He very evidently understood how the cat was dropped.

STOPPING A 'BUS.

MRS. PARTINGTON had watched three quarters of an hour for an omnibus, and she swung her umbrella as one drove up, and the driver stopped his horses near where she stood.

"Now, Isaac," says she, feeling in her reticule for a copper, away down under the handkerchief, and snuff-box, and knitting-work, and thread-case, and needle-book, "be a good boy, dear, while I am gone, and don't cause a constellation among the neighbours, as some boys do, and there's a penny for you; and be sure you don't lay it out extravagantly, now; and be keerful you don't break the windows; and if anybody rings at the door, be sure and see who it is before you open it, because there is so many dishonest rogues about; if any porpoises come a-begging, give 'em what was left of the dinner, Heaven bless 'em, and much good may it do 'em! and —— why, bless me! if the omnibus hasn't gone off, and left me standing here in the middle of the street. Such impudence is without a parable."

Her spectacles gleamed indignantly down the street, after the disappearing 'bus, and, for a moment, anger had the mastery; but equanimity, like twilight, came over her mind, and she waited for the next 'bus, with calmness on her face, and her green cotton umbrella under her arm.

AFTER A WEDDING.

"I LIKE to 'tend weddings," said Mrs. Partington, as she came back from a neighbouring church, where one had been celebrated, and hung up her shawl, and replaced the black bonnet in the long-preserved handbox. "I like to see young people come together with the promise to love, cherish, and nourish each other.

But it is a solemn thing, is matrimony—a very solemn thing—where the pasture comes into the chancery, with his surplus on, and goes through with the cerement of making 'em man and wife. It ought to be husband and wife ; for it a'n't every husband that turns out a man. I declare I shall never forget how I felt when I had the nuptual ring put on to my finger, when Paul said, 'With my goods I thee endow.' He used to keep a dry-goods store then, and I thought he was going to give me all there was in it. I was young and simple, and didn't know till arterwards that it only meant one calico gound in a year. It is a lovely sight to see the young people plighting their trough, and coming up to consume their vows."

She bustled about and got tea ready, but abstractedly she put on the broken teapot, that had lain away unused since Paul was alive, and the teacups, mended with putty and dark with age, as if the idea had conjured the ghost of past enjoyment to dwell for the moment in the home of present widowhood.

A young lady, who expected to be married on Thanksgiving night, wept copiously at her remarks, but kept on hemming the veil that was to adorn her brideship, and Ike sat pulling bristles out of the hearth-brush in expressive silence.

MRS. PARTINGTON IN THE MARKET.

" I WONDER what they mean by a better feeling in the market," said Mrs. Partington, looking up from the newspaper which she was reading, and the problem deeply agitated her mind, revealed in the vibration of her cap-border. Her address was directed to nobody in particular. It was a little private wonder, got up for her own amusement. The market, and the deaths and marriages, were Mrs. P.'s favourite study in the *Weekly Chronicle*, but some of the mercantile phrases were at times imperfectly understood. " I wonder what they mean? I'm shore *I* don't feel any better there, and I don't believe anybody does but the butchers, and that's when they are pocketing the money—things is so dear! But," continued she, brightening up, "I should like to see the trade embracing ten hogsheads of tobacco, that I see here printed about. That must have been a real tetching sight." She thought of Paul, and the association brought out the cotton handkerchief with the Constitution and Guerriere upon it, and she discontinued.

PARTINGTON PHILOSOPHY.

BEFORE the railroad company bought and tore down the Partington mansion, and uprooted and overturned the old family shrines without regard to their sacredness—the Vandals!—turning the good old heart that worshipped there out upon the world to seek new ties amid new scenes, it was Mrs. Partington's delight to gather friends about her at Thanksgiving time, and the time-honoured season passed very happily. Amid the festivities her benignity would beam with such a radiance, that the red seed peppers upon the wall looked ruddier in its genial glow, and the bright tin pans upon the shelf seemed brimful of sunshine, and smiled out upon all who looked at them.

There were fine times at the Partington mansion at Thanksgiving, you may depend. She didn't keep Christmas; she was puritanical in her religious notions, and 'tended the Old North meeting-house for a third of a century, and took pride in saying that she had never been to *church*, a nice distinction, which we leave the old folks to make. Christmas was a church holiday, unsanctioned by a governor's proclamation, and she would none of it; she scented in it the garment of the disreputable Babylonish female mentioned in the Apocalypse, and avoided it. But it is Thanksgiving that we are speaking about now——Well, well, what has all this to do with patience?——Have patience, darling, and we'll tell you an instance of patient resignation under disappointment, not surpassed since Newton's dog Diamond committed an incendiary act, and his master gravely informed the quadruped that he was not probably aware of the extent of the damage he had committed, which was doubtless the fact.

It was the custom with Mrs. P. to shut up a turkey previous to Thanksgiving, in order that he might be nice and fat for the generous season. One year the gobbler had thus been penned, like a sonnet, with reference to Thanksgiving, and anticipations were indulged of the " good time coming; " but, alas! the brightest hopes must fade. The turkey, when looked for, was not to be found. It had been stolen away! Upon discovering her great loss, Mrs. P. was for a moment overcome with surprise—disconcerted; but the sun of her benevolence soon broke the clouds away, and spread over her features like new butter upon hot biscuit, and with a smile, warm with the feeling of her heart, she said—"*I hope they will find it tender! I guess we can be thankful on pork and cabbage!*"

"Say, ye severest, what would ye have done"

under such circumstances? You would, perhaps, have raved, and stamped, and swore, and made yourself generally ridiculous, besides periling your soul in the excess of your anger. But Mrs. P. didn't, and there is where you and she differ. She stood calmly and tranquilly, a living lesson of philosophical patience under extreme difficulty. We cite this example that the world may profit by it.

FILIAL DUTY *V.* WASHING POWDER.

"CHILDREN of the present day," sighed the Rev. Adoniram Spaid, as he was visiting Mrs. Partington during the spring anniversaries—" children of the present day, ma'am, sadly ruffle the bosoms of their parents."

He crossed his legs as he spoke, and tied his handkerchief in a hard knot over his knee, at the same time looking at Ike through the back window, as that young gentleman was performing a slack-rope exercise upon the clothes-line, endangering the caps and handkerchiefs that swung like banners in the breeze. Mrs. Partington suspended washing, and looked round at her visitor, at the same time wiping her hands to take a pinch of snuff.

"Yes, sir," she said, " I think so ; but it isn't so bad either as it used to be before the soap-powder was found out."

Mr. Spaid quietly protested that he could not see the relevancy of the remark.

"Why," continued she, inhaling the rappee, and handing the box to the minister, " then it was a great labour to wash and do 'em up ; but now the washing-powder makes it so easy, that the children can rumple bosoms or anything else with perfect impurity. We don't make nothing of it. I consider washing-powder "—holding up a pair of Ike's galligaskins that had just gone through a course of purification—" as a great blessing to mothers."

The minister smiled, and thought what a curious proposition it would be, in the " Society for the Mitigation of Everything,' to recommend washing-powder as an auxiliary to other operative blessings, and thanked Mrs. Partington for the hint.

A SERIOUS QUESTION.

OLD ROGER came down stairs one Sunday morning, with a face unusually animated, and stood, with his hands behind his back, playing nervously with the tails of his coat. The breakfast was waiting for him, the fish-balls were getting cold, the coffee was evaporating; but he didn't seem to care. He leaned over the back of the landlady's chair, and asked her, in a whisper, if she could tell him why a dyspeptic was out of immediate danger when his disease was most distressing. She looked earnestly at the top of the teapot a few moments, and then said that for the life of her she couldn't tell. A curiosity was evinced by the boarders, and they asked what it was. They all gave it up, too. "Why," said he, looking very red, "it is because he can't di-gest then." Drawing his chin within his stock, the old fellow laughed lustily, and in his paroxysm threw his arms around the landlady's neck for support; but she threw them off very indignantly, for the boarders were all looking at her. He then sat down to breakfast with a good appetite.

RATHER A RASCAL.

"MRS. PARTINGTON, your neighbour, Mr. Gruff, is rather irascible, I think," said the new minister on his first visit to the old lady, as he heard Gruff scolding Ike for throwing snow-balls at his new martin-house. Gruff kept a grocery over the way, and was in a constant quarrel with every boy in the neighbourhood. Mrs. Partington looked at the minister through her spectacles inquiringly before she answered.

"*Rather* a rascal!" said she, slightly misapprehending his question, and patting her box affectionately; "yes, indeed I think he is a great rascal! He sold me burnt peas for the best coffee once, and it wasn't weight nuther. When they built our new church, somebody said there was a nave in it, and I know'd in a minute who they meant. Why"——

"I mean," interrupted the minister, blandly, laying his white hand gently on his arm; "I mean that he is quick-tempered."

"O, that's quite another thing—yes, he is very," and she changed the subject. But that word "irascible" ran in her head for an hour after he was gone, and when Ike came in she told him to take down the old Johnson's Decency and find the defamation of it.

THE SENSITIVE MAN SEES A BLOOMER.

THE Sensitive Man came in one day just after dinner, threw himself into a chair, and fainted. After a mug or two of Cochituate water had been dashed in his interesting face, he came to a little, gazed wildly upon the circle that surrounded him, and said, in a sort of unearthly whisper, " Where is she ?" Nobody knew what he meant. The fog, a moment later, rolled from his soul, and he was enabled to explain, with the aid of some slight stimulant.

A crowd in the street had obstructed his path, as he walked pensively along with his eyes cast down. Looking up, a vision of beauty burst upon his ravished sight, and he stood entranced as he gazed upon it ; and, when it passed away with the crowd, he climbed upon an omnibus and watched that object, through his tunneled hand, until it became indistinct and lost in the distance. That object was a BLOOMER! He had long ardently wished for this opportunity. In visions of the night had angels in short dresses and trousers thrust themselves among his sleeping fancies, to the bewilderment of his waking thoughts. It had become the great idea of his mind, and all his other thoughts bowed to this, as did the sheaves of the Israelitish brethren to the sheaf of Joseph of old. He had at last seen a Bloomer. The climax of his earthly desire was attained. The driver of the 'bus, callous to the emotion of his bosom, asked him " what'n thunder he was a-looking at, up there ?" The Sensitive Man made but one step to the ground, so buoyant was he, and he bounded like cork. He could have leaped over the Mansion House. Little boys and sedate passengers stepped back dismayed, and a gentleman in a black coat and white neckcloth looked around anxiously after a policeman. What were policemen to the Sensitive Man ? Those terrific functionaries were nothing ! Even the cold reality of a watch-house floor would be soft as down, could he carry with him the consciousness that he had seen a Bloomer. He looked to see if her passing figure had not left its impression, in aërial portraiture, upon the impalpable atmosphere. He looked upon the pave to detect the print of her charming foot upon the insensate bricks. But she had fled, like some bright exhalation of the morning, and he turned back sorrowing. A coach came high running over him. The tension of his spirit relaxed, enduring only to bring him within the precinct of his vocation, when his too sensitive nature gave out, and the result was as explained above.

And hourly since has he longingly gazed from the window, in ardent hope of seeing again the beauteous vision which had enthralled him, and disappointment,

> ——— "like a worm in the mud,
> Feeds on his damaged cheek."

POWER OF ATTORNEY. \

WHEN the widow Ames had been notified that her share of the Paul Jones prize money would be paid her upon presenting herself at the Dummer Bank, she debated in her own mind,—though the debate never was reported,—whether she should go herself or give a power of attorney to some one else to receive the eleven pounds and tenpence that was her share. In this strait she called on Mrs. Partington, who she knew had authorised a person to settle the Beanville estate for her when the Beanville Railroad had driven her from the homestead.

"Go yourself, dear," said the old lady, bringing the poker down emphatically upon the bail of the tea-kettle, as she was clearing out the ashes from the stove; "don't trust to nobody but yourself, for"—raising the poker,—"if you give anybody power of eternity, depend upon it you won't never see the final conclusion of it."

The poker fell again upon the harmless tea-kettle, which seemed to sing out with reproach for the outrage, and Ike, who was looking slyly into the back window, wondered if Mrs. Ames wasn't sitting on a favourite piece of spruce gum of his, and whether it wouldn't stick her to the chair so that she couldn't get up. It showed that the boy had a reflective turn of mind.

THE NEW DRESS FOR LADIES.

"A NEW custom for ladies!" said Mrs. Partington, when a friend spoke to her about the proposed innovation in dress. The sound of "costume" came to her ear indistinctly, and she slightly misapprehended the word. "A new custom for ladies! I should think they had better reform many of their old customs before they try to get new ones. We're none of us better than we ought to be, and"——

"Costume, ma'am, I said," cried her informant, interrupting her; "they are thinking of changing their dress."

"Well, for my part, I don't see what they want to make a public thing of it for; changing the dress used to be a private matter; but folks do so alter! They are always a changing dresses now, like the caterpillar in the morning that turns into a butterfly at night, or the butterfly at night that turns to a caterpillar in the morning, I don't know which"——

"But," again interrupted her informant, "I mean they are a going to have a new dress,"

"O, they are, are they?" replied the old lady; "well, I'm sure I'm glad on it, if they can afford it; but they don't always think enough of this. A good many can't afford it—they can't! But did you hear of the new apperil for wimmin that somebody is talking about?"

"Why, my dear Mrs. P.," said he, smiling, "that is just what I was trying to get your opinion about."

"Then," returned she, "why didn't you say so in the first place? Well, I don't know why a woman can't be as vertuous in a short dress as in a long one; and it will save some trouble in wet weather to people who have to lift their dresses and show their ankles. It may do for young critters, as sportive as lambs in a pasture; but only think how I should look in short coats and trousers, shouldn't I? And old Mrs. Jones, who weighs three hundred pounds, wouldn't look well in 'em neither. But I say let 'em do just what they please as long as they don't touch my dress. I like the old way best, and that's the long and the short of it."

She here cast a glance at the profile on the wall, as if for its approval of her resolutions; and an idea for a moment seemed to cross her mind that he, the ancient corporal, would not know her, were he to visit sublunar scenes and find her arrayed in the new dress; and her compressed lips showed the determination of her heart to abide by the old costume, and she solemnly and slowly took an energetic pinch of snuff, as if to confirm it.

MATTER OF FACT.

"SHAKSPEARE's well enough," said Mr. Slow, "but he don't come up to my idee of po'try. There is too much of your hifalutin humbug about him. What he says don't seem to 'mount to nothing. As for Falstaff, he's a miserable and disreputable old fellow, and Hamlick's as mad as a bed-bug. Why didn't he knock his old father-in-law over, and done with it, and not make sich a hillibolu about it? Shakspeare isn't what he is

cracked to be, and if he doesn't improve, I wouldn't give two per
cent. for his chance of immortality. Who b'leves this ere, for
instance?

> 'Orpheus' lute was strung with poets' sinews;
> Whose golden touch could soften steel and stones,
> Make tigers tame, and huge levithians
> Forsake unsounded deeps to dance on sand!'

That's all gammon. Poets' sinews, indeed! Dare say 't wasn't
nothin' but catgut ; and as for its softening steel and stones, and
taming tigers, and making levithians dance on the sand, that'ere's
all bosh, and too ridic'lous for any man to b'leve."

Mr. Slow looked fearfully oracular as he said this, and the
subject was suspended.

THE CAT AND KITTENS.

BEFORE Ike dropped the cat, it was a matter of much annoyance to Mrs. Partington, upon coming down stairs one morning,
to find a litter of kittens in her Indian work-basket, beside her
black Sunday bonnet, and upon the black gloves and handkerchief, long consecrated to grief. Ike had left the basket uncovered,
during a search for some thread to make a snare to catch a pigeon
with. Her temper was stirred by the circumstance, as what good,
tidy housekeeper's would not have been by such an occurrence?

"I'll drownd 'em," said she, "every one of 'em! O, you
wicked creatur!" continued she, raising her finger, and shaking
it at the cat; "O, you wicked creatur, to serve me such a
trick!"

But the cat, happy in the joys of maternity, purred gladly
among her offspring, and looked upon the old lady, through her
half-closed eyes, as if she didn't really see any cause for such a
fuss.

"Isaac," said the dame, "take the big tub, and drown them
kittens."

There was determination in her eye, and authority in her tone,
and Ike clapped his hands as he hastened to obey her.

"Stop, Isaac, a minute," she cried, "and I'll take the chill off
the water; it would be cruel to put 'em into it stone-cold."

She took the steaming kettle from the stove, and emptied it
into the tub, and then left the rest to Ike. But she reproached
herself for her inhumanity long afterwards, and could not bear to
look the childless cat in the face, and many a dainty bit did that
injured animal receive from her mistress. Mrs. Partington, per-

haps, did wrong, as who hasn't at some period of life ? Perfection belongeth not to man or woman ; and we would throw this good pen of ours into the street, and never take another in our fingers, could we pretend that Mrs. Partington was an exception to this universal rule.

A POINT SETTLED.

DR. DIGG—for whose researches the world can never be grateful enough—has been studying out the genealogy of the great family of Co., which occupies such a distinguished mercantile position. This family is scattered the world over, and almost every sign in every city bears the name of one of them as partner. He traces their genealogy back to Jericho, of Palestine (modern Jeremiah Co., or, for shortness, Jerry Co.), whom we find frequently mentioned in ancient books. The doctor expresses the belief that the exclusive business habits of the family may be attributed to their Jewish extraction.

MORAL TRAINING.

"MORAL training," said Mrs. Partington, "is the best arter all." She had heard some one in the omnibus speaking of moral training, and her benevolence gave it into the charge of memory until she got home, and memory revolved it, and pondered it, and reviewed it, and fancy construed it to mean something about the military training that was to come off the next day.

"I hope it will be a moral training, I'm shore," said she, "for I see the General is to be there in his new suit, and I hope they'll make their revolutions well before him. I do admire the millintery, where the sogers in their fancy unicorns look jest like a patchwork quilt. They wasn't moral trainings in old times, when men put ' enemies into their heads to steal away their hats,' as Mr. Smooth, the schoolmaster, used to say Your Uncle Paul had a good deal of millintery sperrit sometimes, Isaac."

Ike had remained very quiet while she was speaking.

"What upon airth are you doing there, Isaac?" cried she.

The young gentleman readily told her he was painting a horse, at the same time displaying an animal, nominally of that description, done beautifully in blue, which he appeared to look on with much satisfaction.

"But what are you painting it with? As true as I'm alive, you've got your Uncle Paul's tompion that he used to wear in his cap so long ago, and you're using up all my bluing.!"

That tompion, saved for so many years, to be used for such a purpose! Ah, Ike, Ike! we fear the old lady will have sad times with thee yet. Why didst thou, yester even, secrete the large ball of yarn for thine own purposes, which to-morrow she will seek in vain? Say, why?

HAIR-DRESSING.

"WHAT a queer place this Boston is!" said Mrs. Partington, when she first came here from the country. "I was walking along the street just now, and saw on a sign 'Hair-Dressing.' 'Something like guano, I guess, for the hair,' said I to myself. 'I declare, I'm a good mind to look at some.' So I went in and asked a dear, pretty young man, smelling as sweet as catnip, to let me look at some of his *hair manure*,—I wanted to be as polite as possible. Gracious! how he started at me, just as if I'd a been a Hottenpot, or a wild Arad. 'I mean your hair-*dressing*,' said I.

"'O, ah, yes!' said he; 'set down here in the big chair, mem,—scratch, perhaps, mem!'

"'Scratch,' said I, completely dumfounded; 'you saucy fellow! I can do all my own scratching, and some of your'n, too, if you say that agin,—scratch, indeed!'—and I went right down the stairs."

She never before had hinted that she stood in need of any hair tonic, though everybody knew that she had worn a wig for twenty years.

MRS. PARTINGTON says that it makes no difference to her if flour is dear or cheap, she always has to pay the same price for half-a-crown's worth.

AURIFEROUS MEDITATIONS.

"GOLDEN airs of Californy," said Mrs. Partington, as she read in the *Post* an advertisement of some new music; "such airs, I should think, would be very replenishing, and I wish a draft of 'em would blow this way. What a country that Califarny is!"

murmured she, in a half reverie, in which golden visions, like the sunshine reflections on the kitchen wall, from her teacup, were dancing through her brain. " What a queer thing! where gold is so plenty they pick it up in quarts on American Forks,—Connetticut ones, I dare say ; but spoons, I should think, would be a good deal better." Of course it would. Strange that the miners did'nt think of this in the first place. Many a valuable suggestion of hers has benefited the world ; though the world was not aware of its indebtedness until she said, " I always thought so ; " and this coming late, she never got the credit for it.

IKE AND THE ORANGES.

" I can't conceive," said Mrs. Partington, standing up on tiptoe, and pushing aside the antique wash-bowl that stood on the front shelf in the old cupboard in the corner, and rattling the papers of seeds, and the teacups, and the plates, and looking into the dark corners, and feeling in, also, to be certain. When she said she " couldn't conceive," it was but part of the sentence that she wished to speak; the earnestness of her search had suspended the remainder it.

" I can't conceive where those oranges are," said she, " that the young ladies sent me—Heaven bless 'em !—they were so good to lucubrate the throat with when it's dry and hot with the information that comes with a cough. It is strange where they have gone. If I believed in superhumorous things I should say the spirits had got 'em; but they wouldn't take mine when they could go so easy where they grow and get as many as they want."

She stopped her search amid the dust, and regaled her nose with dust of a more fragrant character.

" What are you doing, Isaac ?" said she, as she saw him forming a star out of an orange upon the closet door, and using up her pump tacks. The boy pointed to his handiwork, and the delight she felt for his genius blinded her eyes to the possibility of how he might have come by the oranges.

PATRIOTISM.

A Yankee gentleman, convoying a British friend around to view the different objects of attraction in the vicinity of Boston, brought him to Bunker Hill. They stood looking at the splendid shaft, when the Yankee said,

" That is the place where Warren fell."

" Ah!" replied the Englishman, evidently not posted up in local historical matters; " did it hurt him much?"

The native looked at him, with the expression of fourteen Fourth of Julys in his countenance. " Hurt him!" said he, "he was *killed*, sir."

" Ah! he was, eh?" said the stranger, still eyeing the monument, and computing its height, in his own mind, layer by layer; " well, I should think he would have been, to fall so far."

The native tore his hair, but it gave him a good opportunity to enlarge upon the glorious events connected with the hill, and the benefits therefrom flowing to our somewhat extensive country, and he soon talked himself into good-humour.

DULL BUSINESS.

A LONG time ago, in an old town we wot of, there lived a man of humble means—there are some poor people there now—and, in pity for his need, he was made sexton of the church of which he was a member. The times were dull, his salary was low, and he found it hard work to make both ends meet. He called upon the members of the church, but they could not or would not do anything for his relief. As a last resort he called upon the minister, and told him his troubles, and how hard he found it to get along. The minister heard his story; but, instead of relieving his wants, or telling *him* how to do it, went to arguing with him about the unreasonableness of his complaint.

" Why," says he, " don't you have, besides your salary, a number of perquisites? Are you not paid for ringing the bell on the Fifth of November, and other public celebrations? And are you not paid, too, for your services at funerals, when any occur in our society?"

" True," said the dolorous sexton, looking up solemnly; " but I have little hope from this source; for, confound it, none of our society ever die!"

The poor fellow went away sorrowing, thinking, probably, that Providence was rather hard on him in not killing off half the parish that he might have the profit of burying them.

ANTIQUITY IN A SHOWER.

Mrs. Partington attended the dedication of Mount Hope Cemetery, in Dorchester, and got wet with the rain. No sheltering umbrella was there to hold its broad surface above her venerable head; and the rain, all regardless of her august presence, poured down relentlessly. But we will let her tell the story in her own way.

"The siminary would have been dictated, but, by an imposition of divine Providence, the bottles of heaven were uncorked, and the rains fell as if another delusion was agoing to destroy the world. The lightning blazed horridly, and everybody was filled with constipation. Not a shelter to be had! I tried to lean over and get my bonnet under a gentleman's umbrel, in front of me, and the water all run down into my back like a spout, till I was satiated through and through like an old boot. Cold chills run over me as if I had an ager; and, O dear! look at that bonnet."

Certainly the faded remnant had wilted, the pasteboard that formed the crown had relaxed and shook flabbily as we held it, and irreparable decay seemed written upon it.

"It never will be fit to be seen again!" said she, and we fancied a tone of deeper sorrow in her words, as she looked straight up at the stiff old corporal on the wall, whom this antique crape commemorated. Heaven bless thee, Mrs. Partington! we thought, and felt round our capacious pocket for a crown to leave with her, but, as it usually happens when our benevolence comes on, we found none, and came away with a paper pinned to our coat-tail by that "everlasting Ike."

THE NATIONAL EPIC.

"I can't see through it," said Mrs. Partington, with a reflective nod of her head, and her eyes earnestly bent upon the keyhole of the closet door, as if that were the object she could not see through. She had just learned the report of the committee upon the prize poem proposition of Mr. Latham, and the loss of £100 to the musical genius of the country. "I can't see why somebody couldn't have written an epic poem, when there is so many beautiful epicac poets in the country. Dear me, the older I grow— and I never shall see fifty-seven again—I'm convinced that genius isn't thought half enough of, and that versatanity of talent and great power of versuffocation is'nt rewarded as it ought to be.",

This was said in compliment to Wideswarth, who, it was half suspected, had put in for the prize, and he bowed modestly, as he placed his hand in the vicinity of his heart, and felt in his vest pocket for a tooth-pick.

MRS. PARTINGTON AND THE MAINE LIQUOR BILL.

MRS. PARTINGTON was in the gallery of the House of Representatives when the Maine liquor law was under discussion. The member from Cranberry Centre was very attentive to the old dame, and replied to her questions concerning the Maine liquor law, and spoke of the various provisions of the bill. "Provisions!" said the kind old dame, tapping her box gently, "I never heerd there was any provisions mentioned in the bill; though I dare say there is, for Paul used to say that give old Mr. Tipple a pint of rum, it would be vittals and drink and house-rent for a week; and I b'lieve it was so, for, only give him rum enough, he'd never ask for bread. I remember, too," continued the old lady, raising her voice, as she saw Mr. Batkins about to interrupt her—"they used always to put rum and tobacco into their provision bills, in old times, when they went a-fishing, and I s'pose this putting provisions into the liquor bill is 'bout the same thing." She looked at Mr. Batkins, and smiled, as she saw him look smilingly at her, and they both smiled at each other.

"The provisions meant, mem," said the member, impressively, "are provisions of law."

"Ah!" replied the old lady, musingly, as she took the third pinch, and handed the box to Mr. Batkins, "yes, yes, I've heerd of folks bein' bread to the law afore, though a good many of 'em is more like vegetables. But "——— Here the Speaker's mallet attracted her attention, and she listened to the reading of part of the liquor bill, watching carefully for the items. "Is *that* the liquor bill?" asked she, in an incredulous tone, of her friend, the member; "is that it?" He assured her that it was. "Well," continued she, as she rose to go, "I must say that I never see a bill made out in that way afore."

Mr. Batkins handed her out, and she remarked to Mr. Verigreen, whom she met on the stairs, that she had come to hear the liquor bill, and they were reading a new chapter, that she'd never read, in the book of Acts.

TAKE THINGS EASY.

"I never knowed anything gained by being in too much of a hurry," said Mrs. Partington.   "When me and my dear Paul was married, he was in such a tripidation, that he came nigh marrying one of the bridesmaids instead of me, by mistake.   He was such a queer man!" she continued.   "Why, he joined the fire apartment, and one night in his hurry he put his boots on hind part afore; and, as he ran along, everybody behind him got tripped up.   The papers were full of crowner's quests on broken legs and limbs, for a week afterwards,"—and she relapsed into an abstraction on the ups and downs of life.

CARRIED AWAY WITH MUSIC.

Everybody will remember the organ-grinder's little child, who was carried around, seated upon the instrument his father was tuning, his young heart well satisfied with things as they were, so he enjoyed his musical throne.   We regret to say that this babe of tender years was once made the subject of as cruel a joke as was ever seen in print.   Our friend, old Roger, was concerned in it, too, and with his kind feelings 'tis a wonder he could have done it.   Philanthropos observed old Roger standing upon the sidewalk, good humouredly beating time to a lively air performed by the man of the organ, and observing the dexterity with which he would pick up a cent, and not lose a note.

"Sir," said Philanthropos, "observe the hard fortune of that babe, thus chained to such a destiny—a child with a soul to save, thus risking its safety by breathing continually such abominable airs."

"I know it," said old Roger, in his way; "I know it, and yet the little fellow seems to be entirely carried away with the music."

Philanthropos immediately left him.

MRS. PARTINGTON IN TROUBLE.

"Trying the French sea-steamer!" said Mrs. Partington, as she read in the foreign news an account of trial-trips made by the French steamships.   She has always had a deep interest in the French, since Mr. Lay Martin, as she calls Lamartine, has been driven out of the provisional government, and the people have got to go back to frog soup again.   "What can they be going to try them for?"

E

continued she. "I never knowed that steamboats could be arranged for murders and such things before, though I don't see no reason why they shouldn't, seeing so many murders come from their arrangements. And I wish they'd try 'em all before they do the mischief, and condemnation 'll be a warning to 'em, just as it would if we could try all of the murderers, and hang 'em off aforehand, and save the lives of their innocent victims. Isaac!" she screamed, as a snow-ball struck the window, "don't throw your snow this way!" and she rushed out to save her glass. Alas! she was a moment too soon, for a snow-ball struck her cap as she issued from the door, tore it from her head, and bore it, with its strings hanging down, far from her. Her hair, all unconfined, danced madly in the wind, and Mrs. Partington for a moment looked every witch way. Virtue is of little account unless it be tried, nor is patience. Mrs. Partington calmly "digested" her cap on her head, and went in.

INFLUENZA.

"I DECLARE, I b'lieve I'm going to have the influwednesday," said Mrs. Partington, tenderly enveloping her nose in her cotton bandanna, previous to a blast that would have done credit to Sam Robinson's stage-horn in the old time. "'Tis a dreadful feelin' to have your head as big as a bucket of water, and your nose dropping like the eaves, and your flesh all creepy with cold pimples, like a child with the mizzles. Paul's sister's child, she that married with a Smith, had the distemperature so bad, that they had to put cork stoppers in his nostrils to keep his brains from running out!"

She was here "brought-up" suddenly with a fit of coughing; the knitting-work was laid by for the night, and she went up stairs with a hot brick for her feet, and a little preparation of something hotter for her stomach.

AN ANSWER.

"WHAT do they call them dancers the *corpse de ballet* for?" asked Mr. Verigreen of old Roger, at the theatre. The old fellow was watching them intently from the parquette, with a double magnifying opera-glass, and didn't wish to be disturbed, but answered :—"Because no *live* dancers can jump half so high as they can."

MUTTON CUSTARD.

"As regards this mutton custard," said Mrs. Partington, as she held up the spoon with which she was stirring the preserves, and let the treacle trickle back into the kettle in syrupticious ropiness, and stirred it again till the little yellow eyes that bubbled on the top seemed to snap and wink at Ike, who was sitting whittling a stick and looking intently at the operation, till his mouth watered again. "Mutton custard!" and she smiled as the idea stole across her mind, like the shadow of a cloud in summer over a green meadow full of dandelion blossoms and buttercups. "Some new regiment for sick people, I dare say; but I hope it'll be better than the custards that Widow Grudge used to make for the poor, God bless 'em! with one egg to a quart of milk, and sweetened with molasses, and thought that Heaven itself was too small an enumeration for what she had done. But mutton custard!"—

"It is Martin Koszta," said Ike, who had read the name to her in the *Post* of that individual when he arrived in Boston; "Koszta, the Hungarian."

"Well," continued she, "it might have been worse, as the girl said when she kissed the young minister by mistake in the dark entry, for her cousin Betsey,—a mistake is no haystack, Isaac."

Isaac silently admitted the truth of the remark, as he thrust the stick he had been whittling into the kettle, and then made a drawing of the equatorial line across both cheeks in warm molasses.

MRS. PARTINGTON ON THE "RELIGIOUS TEST."

"THE religious taste among politicians!" exclaimed Mrs. Partington, as her opinion was asked on the great question that was then agitating the people of New Hampshire; and she smiled incredulously as she answered, "I never heerd that they had any religious taste at all, nor religious feeling, nuther, for that matter. We see that all the politicians this'ere way that ever had any religion has give it all up. There is Parson Trot, who used to compound the Gospel up in the old church, has come out a politicioner, and where is his religious taste, now, I should like to know? and there's lots just like him"——

"But, dear madam," quoth the interrogator, blandly, "I didn't mean *taste*,—it was test that I spoke about."

She inhaled a large thumb and finger full of her favourite

before she spoke. "Their testiness," said she, "is quite another thing, and none of 'em a'n't no better'n they ought to be."

The inquirer left, decidedly impressed with the originality and truth of her remark.

MRS. PARTINGTON'S IDEA OF HUMOUR.

"WHAT is your opinion of the humour of Hawthorne, Mrs. Partington?" asked a young neighbour that had been reading "Twice-Told Tales."

"I don't know," said she, looking at him earnestly; "but if you have got it, you'd better take something to keep it from striking in. Syrup of buckthorne is good for all sort of diseases of that kind. I don't know about the humour of Hawthorne, but I guess the buckthorne will be beneficious. We eat too much butter, and butter is very humorous."

There was a slight tremour in his voice, as he said he would try her remedy, and a smile might have been perceived about his mouth next day, when she asked him with a solicitous air and tone, how his humour was.

MRS. PARTINGTON ON EXTRADITION.

"EXTRADITION of Sims!" said Mrs. Partington, as she paused a moment before the bulletin board of the *Commonwealth*, during the great excitement; "I don't see what they want with an extra edition of Sims for, when they had so much trouble in getting off the first one!"

"'Eere's the *Commonwealth*, fourth edition!" bawled a news-boy in her ear.

She raised her umbrella with a menacing air, for the noise was strange to her, when her good genius stayed her hand; the umbrella—the old green cotton one—descended gently as a snow-flake, and the kind old lady invested two coppers, American currency, in a last week's paper which the urchin chanced to have on hand.

INDIGNATION MEETING.

THE enforcement of the law requiring our canine friends and fellow-citizens to wear collars about their necks—a servile mark, which no dog of spirit could for a moment consent to wear—caused, as might be supposed, much growling among them; and many teeth were shown, and much dogged determination was evinced to resist the law. Acting upon this feeling, the more energetic of the Caninites went round among their brethren, counselling them to withstand the law, and telling them, besides, that the rights of universal puppydom were in their keeping, and asking them, in tones of earnest entreaty, if they would see those rights sacrificed without a struggle.

This appeal was effectual, and a meeting was forthwith assembled at the old slaughter-house, on the Isle of Dogs, to discuss the great question of resistance. It was composed chiefly of dogs whose necks had never chafed with the ignominious badge of ownership; of hard-faring dogs, bone-gnawing dogs; of dogs not nursed in the lap of luxury or pampered by the indulgence of favouring masters; none of the silk-eared and soft-footed aristocracy; but there were the Huge Paws from Rosemary Lane, the Shagbarks from the North, and the Tough and Roughers from St. Giles, and many of minor note. Not a smile marked their meeting, not a tail wagged, not a bark disturbed the stillness, and anybody with half an eye could see that each heart was nerved with mighty resolution.

The meeting was organised by the choice of CÆSAR, the biggest dog present, for president; and PLATO, a lean dog in specs, who had been very active in getting up the meeting, and who was known to be an excellent reporter, was appointed scribe. Some said, in an under tone, aside, that the scribe had nominated himself, but his well-known modesty precluded the possibility of this, and it may be set down as a slander.

The chairman, on taking his seat, stood up, and, after wagging his tail in silence for some moments, expressive of his deep emotion, he then proceeded to make a speech describing the object of the meeting, characterised by all the profundity, eloquence, brilliancy, and power, that has rendered the name of Cæsar immortal, and that has more or less marked the efforts of every chairman of every meeting since, when the memory of man or dog knoweth not the contrary. We regret very much that we have not this great speech to print. In recommending union in their action, he related an original anecdote about an old man and his sons and a bundle of sticks, which was received with tremendous applause.

There was a struggle for the floor as the chairman ceased, and, amidst much yelping, it was assigned to CATO, an old setter, who called upon his hearers to keep cool and not be in too much of a hurry; they would accomplish more by masterly inactivity than by thrusting their necks in the way of danger; they must remember the conduct of an ancient member of their race—he must refer to it, although it was humiliating to think that a dog should be such a fool—who dropped a piece of beef he had in his mouth for its shadow in the water. Prudence, with both eyes wide open tight, would remove them out of the way of trouble; as a last word, he would advise them to lay low and look out for bricks—a species of dog-bane inimical to canine constitutions.

A heavy, old, dark-browed dog, here arose, who commenced to bay violently against the law and those who were enforcing it. He was astonished, he was paralysed, he was dumfounded, to hear dogs counsel coolness in this crisis! "The policemen are upon us! We have already felt our tails within their degrading fingers! I hold them and their leader in detestation! *He!* I would bark at the woman who does his washing, I hate him so! I would point at him in Whitecross-street, though not naturally a pointer! I would show my teeth at him wherever I met him!" His excitement overpowered him, and he sat down.

PONTO, a large, gnarly, hard-looking dog, here arose, and it was doubtful for a time if he could be heard, for the noise and confusion which prevailed among the opposers of the law. He was for law and order. Law was too sacred a thing to be handled without gloves; it was the palladium of our liberty. If the law was oppressive, as it doubtless was, he would suggest, in his reverence for law, that they grin and bear it; if their necks were a little chafed, the evil would be mitigated by the reflection that the law was inviolate. Individual grievance was nothing in comparison with this grand idea. Everything that is legal is right; what is wrong in the individual may become right in law. Did the law require him to fasten the collar upon his own neck or upon the necks of those with whom he was allied, he would not hesitate to do it, in his regard for the law; he would——

He was here pulled down by his tail, when, amid the shaggy hair which thickly covered his neck, a collar was discovered, fitting closely to the skin! Amid the confusion attending this discovery, he sneaked away.

A sandy-haired dog, named CARLO, next took the floor, and snarled ominously as he commenced. He had but few words to say. He would ask if they were going to allow this law to be enforced? For his part he would fill his pockets with pistols, and with a twenty-four-pounder under each arm would he go alone to oppose it!

His remarks produced an immense sensation among the younger portion of the audience. A cry was here made for "Bones." A venerable dog arose, whose appearance excited respect. He gained his feet with much difficulty, and it was perceived that he had a wooden leg, and bore about his person sundry other marks of dilapidation.

"My brethren," said he, when the cheering which had greeted him had subsided, "you have before you but a sorry dog; but such as I am is all that was left over from that fatal tenth of April, when so many of our race were served up cold. I was then young and ardent. At the first howl of danger, I left the bone I was gnawing, and threw myself into the front rank of the defenders of my race. Alas! my friends, I soon found that I was barking up the wrong tree, and discovered, too, that canine sagacity, however good it might be in saving children from drowning, or worrying cats, could never cope with humanity armed with clubs and actuated by the love of money. In a bloody fray my leg was broken with an ignominious brick; in another my termination was curtailed; in another my right eye closed in darkness on the world for ever. With this view of the power of man, and of our own weakness, I would counsel caution—submission, even—for the present, resting in the assurance of the fulfilment of the ancient prophecy of the good time coming, when 'every dog shall have his day!' when, basking in the broad sunshine of beneficent law, we may catch flies in peaceful security, fearing not the butcher's art, fearing not the urchins' mischief, who, so reckless of our feelings, persist in ornamenting our extremities with cast-off culinary utensils."

This speech produced a great sensation, awakening the president, who had fallen asleep during the pathetic part of it; and a few sensitive pups near the door were so deeply affected that they had to go out and take a little whine to restore their strength. The scribe, who had prepared a series of resolutions before he came, concluded not to submit them, and let them drop back in his pocket, to read some other time to private admirers; and the meeting dissolved

HOW TO GET OUT OF AN OMNIBUS.

GIVE a loud and sudden roar at the same instant you start from your seat to make for the door. The motion of the coach will afford you an excellent opportunity of testing your powers of navigation, and will not in the least annoy you, although it may be annoying to those whose corns you tread on. If you are timid of falling into the laps of your fellow-passengers, incline your body forward, as if about commencing to swim, and place your hands upon projecting knees on each side, until you are at a right distance from the door, and then make a sudden and energetic plunge at it, as if attempting to carry it by storm. We have seen a lady attempt this mode of egress, and, by skilful management, contrive to sit on seven masculine laps before she reached the door. It saves time to start a trifle before roaring; you might lose a full sixteenth of a minute by waiting for the coach to stop, and that is something where " time is money," and money is two per cent. a month!

A LITERAL CONSTRUCTION.

" PREACHERS," said a reverend gentleman, "should be careful, in doing their Master's service, never to exceed their commission, or take anything but the Bible into their mouths."

" Bless me !" thought Mrs. Partington, as he said this; " I don't see how he could find room for anything more very well; though some mouths are a great deal larger than others. I remember my poor Paul and his brother were digging a cellar once, when Paul threw some dirt in his brother's mouth. 'Paul,' says he, 'you've filled my mouth half full of dirt.' His brother had a very big mouth. ' Have I?' said Paul; ' well, just spit it outside, and we shan't have any more to dig.' Ah, Paul was such a queer man! He was the beatermost creatur."

What a joyous gleam shot from her specs as this reminiscence crossed her mind, giving the very iron of the bows the semblance of gold in its light! But the reflection cost her the whole of the fourthly.

QUESTION ANSWERED.

" WHERE is the fire?" asked Mrs. Partington of a fireman, from an upper window, as the bells were waking the night with their clangour.

"In ——," was the ungallant response, naming the hottest title of perpetual warmth. "Dear me!" said the old lady, not comprehending him; "is it so far off? I wish it was nearer for your sake! But he'll get there soon," she muttered to herself, "if he goes on as he does now;" and she went to sleep again, invoking blessings on the guardians of public safety.

A WHOLESOME LESSON.

"A DOG is a very singular animal," said the owner of Fido to old Roger, after they had marked the affectionate gambols of the faithful creature, who now, in weariness, had come to lie at his master's feet; "a very singular animal. Now you see I will flog him severely (suiting the action to the word); and now you see him licking my hand in return."

Old Roger was moved.

"Yes," said the old man severely, "and were I the dog I would give you a different sort of licking from that. He is the noblest animal of the two, and ought to change places with you. Let me tell you, sir, that a man who by a mere accident occupies .the superior position, and out of pure wantonness abuses the power he may possess, or presumes upon that power to hurt the helpless, is a scoundrel, sir! That dog, there, is a king to him."

And the old man turned away, leaving Fido and his master to experience perhaps the benefit of the lesson. There is a moral in it.

PERHAPS TRUE.

A PAPER begins a paragraph eulogistic—"Price, the immortal friend of mothers," &c. We are assured, by a friend at our elbow that knows, that price is no object with some mothers; and that however much it may be pretended that Price is the mother's friend, it is a notorious fact that price is obnoxious to fathers.

OLD ROGER'S NEW HAT.

"For Heaven's sake, old woman, get off my hat!" said Roger at the concert, as he saw a two hundred and fifty pounder settle on his new ventilated castor. *Old woman!* It was an ungallant expression, but the circumstance would seem to justify it. A new hat was a new era in his existence, and this was one of the latest. Recovering himself, and pressing over his knee as best he might his crushed tile, the wrinkles but too apparent, he calmly continued, "I wouldn't object to your trying it on, ma'am, were there the least chance of its fitting ; but it is evident that it isn't large enough. *I* never saw a hat worn in that way before, and *I* don't want to furnish one to experiment upon, either."

The hat was put on, but how like an apothecary's 'prentice long indented it looked, contrasted with its previous fair proportions ! The opera is very destructive to hats, especially where they throw them at the singers.

CHRISTMAS REFLECTION.

" I wish you a merry Christmas
And a happy New Year,
With your stomach full of money,
And your pocket full of beer,"

yelled Ike, as he skipped into Mrs. Partington's kitchen, where the old dame was busily engaged in cooking breakfast on Christmas morning.

"Don't make such a noise, dear," said the kind old lady, holding up her hand: "you give me a scrutinising pain in my head, and your young voice goes through my brains like a scalpel knife. But what did the good Santa Cruz put in your stocking, Isaac?"

And she looked at him with an arch and pleased expression, as he took out of his pocket a jacknife, and a humtop painted with gaudy colours. Ike held them up joyously, and it was a sight to see the two standing there, she smiling serenely upon the boy's happiness, and he grateful in the possession of his treasures.

"Ah!" said she, with a sigh, "there's many a home to-day, Isaac, that Santa Cruz won't visit, and many a poor child will find nothing in his stocking but his own little foot!"

It might have been a grain of the snuff she took, it might have been a floating mote of the atmosphere, but Mrs. Partington's eyes looked humid, though she smiled upon the boy before her, who stood trying to pull the cord out of her reticule to spin his new top with,

REFLECTION ABOUT MOSQUITOS.

"THERE! now I hope you've got it, you everlastin' torment!" said Mrs Partington, angrily giving Margaret, her young neigh-bour, who was in spending the evening with her, a smart slap on her forehead, and nearly throwing her from her chair; at the same time knocking the Britannia lamp from the table by her violent motion.

"What's the matter?" inquired Margaret, alarmed; for such conduct was very unusual, and the oil from the lamp had marred her new calico.

"It's only a pesky musketeer, dear," said the old lady, re-lighting the lamp; "it's only a musketeer, and I can't see the use of 'em, the tormenting creaturs! Thy say the Lord makes everything for some good purpose; and so I think that these sort of annoysome reptiles must be made by somebody else, I do." -

The remark may be thought irreverent by some, but the old lady was excited, and the heat of these warm, mosquito-teeming evenings ought to excuse more, even, under such annoyance as she was suffering.

A PASSABLE JOKE.

OLD ROGER was at the concert one evening, and as he sat awaiting the commencement of the performances in a slip where there was room for one more, a gentleman came along, and tap-ping him on the shoulder told him in a whisper that he should like to pass inside of him. Old Roger looked at the stranger a moment; he was a large man, very large.

"Upon my word, sir," said the old fellow, "I don't think you can, for I have just eaten a hearty supper, and from appearances I should judge that you wouldn't sit well on my stomach."

This was said loud enough for people in the adjacent seats to hear, and in an instant eleven double spy-glasses were levelled at him. The gentleman looked very red at first.

"I mean," said he, pointing to the vacant seat, "will you allow me to pass by you to that seat?"

"Certainly, sir," said old Roger gravely, "and I am rejoiced to find that your request is so much more passable than I at first regarded it."

The stranger immediately tendered old Roger his hat, which he magnanimously declined receiving.

A PROCINE EXPOSURE.

"Couldn't you get *young* pork, ma'am, to bake with your beans?" said old Roger, somewhat cynically, as he sat at table one Sunday.

"They told me it was young!" said the landlady.

"Well, it may be so, but gray hair is not a juvenile feature, by any means, in our latitude, ma'am," continued he, fishing up a gray hair, about a foot and a half long with his fork. "He *may* have been young, but he must have lived a very wicked life to be gray so soon."

As he spoke he looked along the table, and a slight emotion was visible among the boarders; and the man who sat opposite, with his mouth full of the edibles with which he had been endeavouring to smother a laugh, grew dark with the effort, and then collapsed, scattering dismay and crumbs amid the nicely-plaited folds of old Roger's shirt-frills.

A NAVE IN THE CHURCH.

"A nave in our church!" screamed Mrs. Partington, as her eye rested on a description of the new edifice, and the offensive word struck terror to her soul; "a nave in our church! who can it be? Dear me, and they have been so careful, too, who they took in,—exercising 'em aforehand, and putting 'em through the catechis and the lethargy, and pounding them into a state of grace! Who can it be?" And the spectacles expressed anxiety. "I believe it must be a slander, arter all. O, what a terrible thing it is to pizen the peace of a neighbourhood deterotating and backbiting, and lying about people, when the blessed truth is full bad enough about the best of us!"

What a lesson is here for the mischief-maker to ponder upon! Truth lent dignity to her words, and gave a beam to her countenance, reminding one somewhat of a sunset in the Fall on a used-up landscape.

Mrs. Partington, one Fourth of July, was much incommoded by the crowd that rushed to see the procession. She said she "didn't see the least need of scrowging so, for she dared say the procession was full long enough to go round."

A QUEER ASSOCIATION.

It was with a strong emotion of wonder, that Mrs. Partington read in the papers that a new wing was to be added to Cambridge Observatory.

"What upon airth can that be for, I wonder. I dare say they are putting the new wing on to take more flights arter comics and such things, or to look at the new ring of the planet Satan,—another link added to his chain, perhaps; and, gracious knows, he seems to go further than he ever did before."

She stopped to listen, as the sounds of revelry and drunkenness arose upon the night air, and she glanced from her chamber over the way, where a red illuminated lantern denoted "Clam Chowder." Why should she look there just at that moment of her allusion to Satan? What connection could there be in her mind between Satan and clam chowder? Nobody was near but Ike, and Isaac slumbered.

THE PUNDIT PUNNED.

Dr. Digg and old Roger were holding an animated conversation upon the subject of California, the Doctor contending that the chances were against the emigrants thither getting recompensed for their trouble; "for," said the Doctor, "the ground is all occupied, and those coming last have small chance of procuring a lucrative field for their operations."

"My dear sir," said old Roger, with animation, "I can assure you it is not so; for I am informed by an intelligent returned Californian, that every man who goes to the mines has his *pick*."

The Doctor, however, still contended for his point, and could not see how it could be possible, and thought old Roger's friend must be mistaken.

PUNCH IN THE HEAD.

Old Sherry came home one night when it was so near morning that the line dividing the night from the morning was legitimately debatable, and having taken an extra glass or two previous to leaving the company he had been with, he was somewhat dull of apprehension, and the houses seemed walking around him unaccountably, and the streets, by some sort of undulatory motion that he had never before noticed, seemed determined to throw him down; but he got home safely.

So far, well; but he had lost his night-key, or it was in the pocket of his other pants, in the wardrobe, within ten feet of the spot where Mrs. Sherry was probably at that time reposing; whose snore he even fancied he heard jarring the latch of the outside door. It must be one or the other, for he felt in his pockets for it in vain. He didn't like to alarm the house, nor the people in it, for a quarter of a century's experience of the quality of Mrs. Sherry's temper, led him to know that her welcome to him, in his present plight, would be more warm than agreeable, even if she consented to let him in at all.

It at last occurred to him that a window in the rear of the house could be opened from the outside, and he at once resolved to gain an entrance in this manner, then creep up stairs to bed, and say nothing to nobody. Accordingly, with this burglarious idea in his mind, he went round to the back of the house. The window was a little above his reach, but he found a barrel somewhere, and by skilful manœuvring got it beneath the window, and elevated himself upon it. He tried to lift the sash, and it slid up easily to the desired height, where he secured it with a stick. Mr. Sherry congratulated himself upon this triumphant achievement under difficulty. The outposts were won—another step, and he would be master of the citadel. Already was his foot raised to take this last step; his head and shoulders were within the window, when the treacherous barrel, losing its equipoise in the exertion Mr. Sherry was making, fell over; his luckless elbow touching the stick that sustained the window, it fell with a crash upon Mr. Sherry's broad shoulders, and he found himself in a trap from which he could not escape.

Mr. Sherry's maiden sister, a romantic damsel of thirty-five, had heard the noise, and as she awaked from her slumber the idea of thieves flashed across her mind. She had been dreaming of brigands and robbers, and the noise occurred just where a heroine was forcibly carried from her paternal home by ruffians in masks! Upon the spur of the moment, she darted into her nephew's chamber, contiguous to hers, and told him, in a big whisper, that robbers were breaking into the house; and added the gratuitous and sanguinary information, that they would all be murdered in their beds!

While she went to impart this gratifying news to the rest of the household, the young man arose, and, without stopping to dress himself, seized a big stick and went stealthily down stairs. He opened the door softly of the room from which the noise proceeded, and, beholding the supposed burglar in the window, the young Sherry gave his parent's head a couple of whacks with the

stick, when a cry from that suffering specimen of suspended animation revealed to the young man who the victim was, and, with
the assistance of the rest of the family, who had now assembled,
the two hundred pounds of old Sherry were soon housed.

Such a lecture as he received! Either the lecture, or the
debauch, or the cane, perhaps the whole combined, gave him a
severe headache the next morning, and he was constrained to
keep his bed. He summoned his son to his bedside, and with an
expression of grave authority he asked the young man if he
didn't think he was a graceless rogue, to be punchin' his parent's
head in the way he did—if he wasn't really ashamed of himself!
The young Sherry made up a mouth, in which much fun blended
with considerable that was serious, and replied that his respected
sire would never have got any punch in his head from him, had
it not been for the punch he had got in his head before he came
home. The old Sherry admitted the corn, and turned over and
slept on it.

MATTER OF FACT AND SENTIMENT.

SAID Augustus, as he gazed from Mrs. Partington's little
window, his finger pensively resting upon a cracked china teapot upon the sill,—" Here is a spot in which to cultivate the
flowers of poesy; here the imagination may soar on unrestricted
wing; here balmy zephyrs, rising from embowering roses, waft
ambrosial sweets "—

" Them is beans planted in the window," said the old lady,
interrupting him. " What you say is very true; there is nothing
better for a sore than balmy-gilead buds in rum; and it's so
handy to have them in a temperance neighbourhood, too, where
people are too good to keep rum in the house themselves, but
leave it all to be berryed of the neighbours. How glad I am
always to have it for 'em! They are so kind, too, always advising
me to give up keeping it in the house; but, dear me, what
would the poor creturs do if I should? I may be committing
sin in keeping it; but a bad use of a thing makes all the trouble
after all."

Augustus was moved; but there was so much of the " earth
earthy " in her remark, that he was silent.

" I should like to know what he meant about emboweling
roses," muttered she to herself; " peppermint would be better if
he has the colic."

She looked at him earnestly, but there seemed no token of
pain, and she forbore to speak.

COMMISERATION FOR CLERKS.

"SHOPKEEPERS is not enough thought of," said Mrs. Partington, after having been out making some purchases. "How they do toil and how they suffer! One dear pretty young man, with a nice black coat on and a gold chain and a starched collar, with a carrivan on his neck, told me with tears in his eyes that he was selling to me at less than he gave for it; and I bought it out of pity, though I knowed I could get it five cents a-yard cheaper next door. Talk about Moses being executed on one string, indeed! These poor creturs are Rogerses, every one of 'em, by the yard-stick, and are all the time a dying."

There's a constant flow of the milk of compassion in her breast-inexhaustible; like the purse of the gentleman in the story, the more that is taken from it the more remains. The allusion to Moses was drawn from an advertisement of a prodigy violinist who was to play a violin solo, from the oratorio of "Moses," upon one string.

THE BOUQUET.

"LOOK here!" exclaimed Mrs. Partington, in a tone of triumph, as she returned from answering the door-bell, bearing in her withered hand a bouquet of generous proportions and exquisite beauty, with her name written in fair characters upon an accompanying card. "Look here, at the bucket of flowers somebody has sent me. How charmingly it smells, as well as looks! And the colours is all blinded together, too, so prettily!"

At this stage of her admiration, a small billet dropped upon the floor.

"And here," she continued, "is a letter besides, written in a beautiful hand, from somebody with ornamental corners." "From your valentine, TIMOTHY TOBY," closed the missive.

She said not another word, took one more inspiration from the "bucket," and busied herself in preparing the large-mouthed honey-bottle for its accommodation. It might have been from the projecting lily spear, it might have been from a grain of subtle maccaboy coming in contact with her eye, and it might have been from some deeper cause, but a tear escaped the area of the right eye of her specs, and stood for an instant in pellucid lustre on her cheek-bone, before passing away through the channels time had worn in her face.

MRS. PARTINGTON ON VENTILATION.

"WE have got a new venerator on our meeting-house," said Mrs. Partington; "but how on airth they can contrive to climb up there to let the execrations go out, is more than I can see into. But it is sich a nice intervention for keeping a house warm!"

"What sort of a ventilator is it?" asked we, anxious to get an inkling of the old lady's philosophy.

"It is one of the Emissary's," replied she, sagely, "and it is ever so much better than Professor Epsom's, because a room is kept so warm and comfortable by it; not the least danger of taking cold from draughts of too fresh air. It will be a great accusation in cold weather."

"But how will it do in summer?" we again asked. The dame, for a moment, was puzzled. She had not thought of this contingency.

"O!" cried she, after a few moments' reflection, aided by the merest trifle of maccaboy, at the same time proffering us the box, "I suppose then they will stop it up altogether, and open the windows."

It was an idea worthy of the profound black bonnet and far-seeing specs before us. She left us then. We watched her from the window, and felt anxious about her rheumatism, as we saw her right foot sink in a puddle, in an attempt to reach a New Road omnibus.

Any one who breathes the suffocating air of our concert rooms, will be reminded of Mrs. Partington's "venerator" for keeping a room warm.

OUR RELATIONS WITH MEXICO.

"Our relations with Mexico!" said Mrs. Partington, contemplatively, and her glance turned upward to the wall, where the portrait of the deceased corporal, in rigid pasteboard, looked straight forward, as if indicating a bee-line of duty that she should follow—a sort of pictorial cynosure to which she always looked for guidance. "Our relations with Mexico!" said she; "some of the poor creaturs, maybe, left there in the late hospitalities, too poor to get back. If I was President Pierce, now, I'd send right away and bring 'em all home by express. The Mexicans had better not trouble any of our relations, I can tell 'em!"

Of course she could tell 'em. There was no doubt of it. Mrs. Sled believed she could, and Ike, who was busy in transformin the old lady's new-clothes-stick into a bat, didn't say a word. If there is a weakness in Mrs. P.'s character—and, as a chronicler, we should be false to our trust to say that there was not—that weakness is love for her relations, continually manifesting itself in blue yarn stockings and souchong tea.

THE FIRST OF APRIL.

" I NEVER see the like!" said Mrs. Partington, as she slammed to the front door, with a noise and jar that set everything to dancing in the house, and the timid crockery stood with chattering teeth upon the little "buffet" in the corner. It was wrong in her to say she had never seen the like, for this was the fifth time that she had been called to the door by a violent ringing, within half an hour, and had found no one there. Hence anger, so rarely an occupant of her mind, but so justifiable now, prompted the slamming of the door and the remark, " I never see the like!"

It was the first of April, and the occurrence was the more annoying for this reason. She stood still by the door and watched stealthily for the intruder; tapped her box easily and regaled her olfactories with a dusty oblation, and held still. The peal of the bell again startled her by its vehemence. She opened the door and looked out, but no one was to be seen. As she turned away, a string attached to the bell-wire, extending from the bannister, met her gaze, and, sitting quietly upon the stairs, with a grin on his face that had a world of meaning and a world of fun in it, sat *Ike!* How the spectacles sparkled in the rays of her indignation! She went for the rod, which had long rested on the shelf; but it had been manufactured three days before into an arrow by Ike, and, as the chance of finding it diminished, her anger cooled like hot iron in the air, and the rogue escaped.

AN INQUIRY ANSWERED.

" DOES Isaac manifest any taste for poetry, Mrs. Partington?" asked the schoolmaster's wife, while conversing on the merits of the youthful Partington. The old lady was basting a chicken that her friends had sent her from the country.

" O, yes!" said the old lady, smiling; " he is very partially fond of poultry, and it always seems as if he can't get enough of it." The old spit turned by the fire-place in response to her answer while the basting was going on.

"I mean," said the lady, "does he show any of the divine afflatus?"

The old lady thought a moment. "As for the divine flatness, I don't know about it. He's had all the complaints of children, and when he was a baby he fell and broke the cartridge of his nose; but I hardly think he's had this that you speak of."

The roasting chicken hissed and sputtered, and Mrs. Partington basted it again.

BAILED OUT.

"So, our neighbour, Mr. Guzzle, has been arranged at the bar for drunkardice," said Mrs. Partington; and she sighed as she thought of his wife and children at home, with the cold weather close at hand, and the searching winds intruding through the chinks in the windows and waving the tattered curtain like a banner, where the little ones stood shivering by the faint embers. "God forgive him and pity them!" said she, in a tone of voice tremulous with emotion.

"But he was bailed out," said Ike, who had devoured the residue of the paragraph, and laid the paper in a pan of liquid custard that the dame was preparing for Thanksgiving, and sat swinging the oven door to and fro as if to fan the fire that crackled and blazed within.

"Bailed out, was he?" said she; "well, I should think it would have been cheaper to have pumped him out, for, when our cellar was filled, arter the city fathers had degraded the street, we had to have it pumped out, though there wasn't half so much in it as he has swilled down."

She paused and reached up on the high shelves of the closet for her pie plates, while Ike busied himself in tasting the various preparations. The dame thought that was the smallest quart of sweet cider she had ever seen.

HAVE YOU GOT A BABY ?

A BACHELOR friend of ours was riding, upon a time, through the state, when he overtook a little girl and boy, apparently on their way to school. The little girl appeared to be five or six years old, and was as beautiful as a fairy. Her eyes were lit up with a gleam of intense happiness, and her cheeks glowed with the hues of health. Our bachelor looked at her for a moment

admiringly. She met his glance with a smile, and with an eager
voice saluted him with—

"Have you got a baby?"

He was struck aback by the question, and something like a
regret stole over his mind as he looked upon the animated and
beautiful little face before him.

"No," he answered.

"Well," she replied, drawing her tiny form proudly up, "*we
have*," and passed on, still smiling, to tell the joyous news to the
next one she might meet.

What a world of happiness to her was concentrated in that one
idea—the baby! And in her joy she felt as if all must have the
same delight as herself; and it was a matter of affectionate pride
to her, that lifted her little heart above the reach of ordinary
care; for in the baby was her world, and what else had she to
crave? Such was the reflection of our friend, and he remembered it long enough to tell it to us.

A HOME TRUTH.

"WHAT a to-do they make about treating the slaves bad at
the south!" said Mrs. Partington; and everybody strained their
ears to catch an opinion that perhaps was fraught with the destiny
of millions. There was a slight tremour in her voice, a sort of
rumbling before the "bustin'" of the volcano, and her eye looked
troubled as a lake by a fitful gust. "What a to-do they do make
about it, to be sure! But some of our folks don't do much better.
I know a poor old coloured man here in Boston that they treat
jest like a nigger. People a'n't no better than scribes, pharisees,
and hippogriffs, that say one thing and do another."

There is truth in thy remarks, O most estimable Mrs. P.!
Our philanthropy, we fear, if weighed in the just balance, would
be found often sadly wanting.

A SEASONABLE PUN.

"FINE gloves, them!" said old Roger, as he held out his hands,
encased in a new pair he had just bought. An assent was expressed. "But," continued he, "can you tell me why a man is
more likely to be taken in, while buying gloves in winter than in
summer?" They couldn't. "I'll tell you, then; it's because
they are more apt to get worsted."

VARICOSE VEINS.

" WHAT is the matter with Mrs. Jewks, doctor ? " asked Mrs. Partington, as Dr. Bolus passed her house. She had been watching for him for half an hour through a chink in the door, and people who detected the end of a nose thrust out of the chink aforesaid, stopped an instant to look at it, strongly inclined to touch it and see what it was.

" She is troubled with varicose veins, mem," replied the doctor, blandly.

" Do tell ! " cried the old lady ; " well, that accounts for her very coarse behaviour, then ; and it isn't any fault o' her'n, arter all, poor woman, 'cause what is to be will be, and if one has very coarse veins what can one expect ?   Ah, we are none of us better than we ought to be ! "

" Good morning, mem," said Dr. Bolus, as he turned away, and the old lady shut the door.

" No better than we ought to be ! "   What an original remark, and how candid the admission !   The little front entry heard it, and the broad stair that led to the chamber heard it, and Ike heard it, as he sat in the kitchen, daubing up the old lady's Pembroke table with flour paste, in an attempt to make a kite out of a choicely-saved copy of the *Morning Herald*.   " We are no better than we ought to be "—generally.

MRS. PARTINGTON ON VACATION.

" FIVE weeks' vexation in August ! " said Mrs. Partington, when she heard that the school had a vacation for five weeks ; " five weeks' vexation !   It is a trying season for mothers, and wearing and tearing to their patience and the jackets and trousers of the children.   Talk about the relaxing from study !   I don't believe it's half as bad as the green apples they get in the country.   But I do love to see the little dears enjoying themselves, frisking about like pigs in clover, as happy as the day is long.   What an idea of freedom there is in a little boy with his face and hair full of molasses and fun and good-nature !   Be still, you good-for-nothing ! " cried she, as Ike attempted to take her snuff-box ; " Be still, I say ! "

But it was not in anger ; for she felt in her capacious pocket, and, from away down under her snuff-box, and thimbles, and bone-buttons, and needles, and pin-cushions, and beeswax, she brought up a ball of variegated hues, and smiled as she gave it into his eager hand, and bade him be a good boy.

TORCHLIGHT PATRIOTISM.

"HOORAY! hooray!" yelled Ike, as he dashed in at the front-door with a lighted torch, swinging it over his head, and spattering the oily fluid around upon the tables and chairs, a drop even falling upon the snow-white table-cover that lay folded up on a shelf. The smoke of the torch filled the kitchen, and rolled along the snow-white ceiling in murky volume, to the great annoyance of Mrs. Partington, who always said if there was anything on "airth" that she held in utter "exorescence," it was "ile."

"What's to pay now?" said the dame rising, and she heard, through the floor, the noise made by the "unterrified democracy" in torchlight procession assembled. Paul was a democrat, and her sympathy kept time with the martial music.

"Quite a furor," said we to her as we recognised her. A tremendous cheer interrupted us.

"A few roar," said she, smiling, "I think it is a good many roar. Ah!" continued she, "I do love to see the unclarified democracy in possession, with their torches a blazing and their patrickism a busting."

She felt patriotic. Her face was momentarily lit up with the emotions of her soul and the light of a Roman candle, and then the venerable countenance melted away in the darkness, as the candle, after making a great effort to sustain itself, became exhausted and snuffed itself out.

MRS. PARTINGTON ON SUFFRAGE.

"How these men do talk about exercising their right of sufferings!" said Mrs. Partington; "as if nobody in the world suffered but themselves. They don't think of our sufferings. We, poor creturs, must suffer and say nothing about it, and drink cheap tea, and be troubled with the children, and scour and scrub our souls out; and we never say a thing about it. But a man comes on regularly, once a-year, like a Farmer's Almanac, and grumbles about his sufferings; and it's only then jest to choose an M.P. arter all. These men are hard creturs to find out, and a'n't worth much after you have found 'em out."

This was intended as a lesson to Margaret, who was working Charlotte and Werter on a blue ground, at her side; but Margaret had her own idea of the matter, and remained silent.

DOWN WITH THE TYRANT.

"HA! ha! Down with the tyrant! Death to the Spaniard!" shouted Ike, as he rushed into the kitchen, brandishing Paul's old artillery sword that had hung so long on the wall. He struck an attitude, and then struck the upright portion of the stove funnel till it rung with the blow, and Mrs. Partington, with amazement on her countenance and the glass lamp in her hand, stood looking at him. Ike had been reading the thrilling tale of the "Black Avenger, or the Pirate of the Spanish Main," and his "intellects," as Sir Hugh Evans might say, were absorbed by the horrible.

"Don't, Isaac, dear," said Mrs. Partington; and she spoke in a gentle, but firm tone. "You are very scarifying, and it don't look well to see a young boy acting so. It comes, I know, of reading them yellow cupboard books. You should read good ones; and, if you won't touch that again, I will let you have my big Bible, King James's aversion, with the beautiful pictures. I declare, I don't know what I shall do with you if you carry on so. I am afraid I shall have to send you to a geological cemetery to get the old sancho out of you."

The point of the sword was lowered as it was making a passage for a dark spot in the centre panel of the door; the eye of the boy, so fiercely lit by the spirit of the "Black Avenger," became mild and laughing, as he said he was only "making b'lieve," and Mrs. Partington gave him a penny as she disarmed him. What a visible emotion of peanuts became manifest as he grasped the copper and made tracks for the door, and climbed over the snow-drifts to reach the grocer's opposite!

MRS. PARTINGTON AND THE CLERK.

"Is the steamer signified, sir?" asked Mrs. Partington at the telegraph station.

"Yes 'm," replied the clerk, who was busily engaged turning over the leaves of his day-book.

"Can you tell me," continued she, "if the queen's encroachment has taken place yet?"

"Some say she is encroaching all the time," said the clerk, looking pleasantly at the old lady, and evidently pleased with his own smartness.

"That isn't possible," responded the venerable dame; "but," said she to herself, "how could *he* be expected to know about such things? and yet there is no reason why he shouldn't, for all the bars to science, 'notamy and them things, is let down now-a-days, and Natur is shown all undressed, like a puppet-show, sixpence a sight!"

"Good morning, sir," said she, as he bowed her out; and as she passed down the stairs, her mind, grasping the manifold subjects of the telegraph, queen, and facilities in science, became oblivious in a fog.

PEACE INCULCATED.

"Better is a crust of bread and quietness therewith than a stollid ox and strife," said Mrs Partington, as she heard the noise of wrangling in a neighbour's house. It was a Sunday morning, and Ike was cleaning his shoes by the door with the clothes-brush. "Why can't folks live in peace, without distention? How much people have to answer for, that causes animosity in a neighbourhood! Thank Heaven, I've never done anything of the kind that my conscience acquits me of."

With what a feeling this was uttered! And the sunlight came into the window, and looked through her specs down into her soul, and it was as calm there as the bottom of a well, not disturbed by Ike's whistling "Old Dan Tucker" as an accompaniment to his brush.

MRS. PARTINGTON RURALISING.

MRS. PARTINGTON and Ike were huckleberrying in the country, and a large swamp was wearily canvassed to find the quart which she bore in her five-quart pail. She despaired of filling it.

"Look here, aunt," said Ike, in a sort of confidential whisper, "look in there and see what a lot of 'em."

There was a smile upon the face of the boy that betokened mischief, or it might have been a gleam of satisfaction at the prospect of filling the pail; but certainly a smile was round the little mouth, and the eye caught it, and a roguish twinkle like a sunbeam lay sparkling there.

"I see!" said the old lady, and a moment later the log cabin bonnet, borrowed for the occasion, was seen above the tops of the bushes, its restlessness indicating its wearer's activity. Ike remained outside.

Fizz-z-z—Buzz-z-z!—what was that?—a humble-bee as we are a sinner. Another and another. The log cabin was besieged, and Mrs. Partington rushed frantically from the bushes, swinging the tin pail, and crying "Shoo! shoo!" with all her might. It was a trying time for the widow of Corporal Paul. And Ike did not escape, for a big humble-bee attacked him, and he roared heartily with a sting upon his cheek. The laugh disappeared.

At the recital of their troubles at home, people regarded the matter as a trick of Ike's; but how could he have known about the humble-bee's nest being in there? Mrs. Partington avowed that she "never was so frustrated by anything in her born days," and the people believed her. She thinks, notwithstanding the bees, that she would like to have a "villain" in the country, and become an "amatory" farmer.

VENTILATION.

In the course of his rambles in the country, Mr. Spotgam called at a poor-looking house by the road-side, to inquire the whereabouts of a trout brook which he supposed to be in the vicinity. Some pretty children attracted his attention, and he stepped inside the door to play with them, and invest a few coppers in their affection. Their father came in a moment afterwards, and appeared somewhat confused to find a stranger in his humble domicile.

"Warm, sir," said he, wiping his forehead; "wife, throw up the window, and let us have a mouthful of fresh air."

Mr. Spotgam looked at the window about to be thrown up, and saw with pain that every square of glass had been broken out. His mind turned to a nice mathematical calculation, in which he endeavoured to make out the difference between the quantity of air received through an open window and one with no glass in it, and gave it up in despair.

OUT OF PLACE.

"Does your arm pain you much, sir?" asked a young lady of a gentleman who had seated himself near her, in a mixed assem

bly, and thrown his arm across the back of her chair, and slightly
touched her neck,

"No, miss, it does not; but why do you ask?"

"I noticed it was considerably out of place, sir," replied she;
"that's all."

The arm was removed.

LEARNING TO RELISH IT.

WE were surprised to see Mr. Slow at an opera one evening,
Leaning over the back of his seat, we remarked that we had an
impression that he didn't like opera music.

"I never did," said he, "till lately; but I've been eddicating
for it. It can be done. Talk about natur's having all to do with
it! that's all humbug. Natur don't have any more to do with it
than she does with learnin us to eat tomatoes, nor sardines, nor
olives; but by eddication we come to like 'em. That's jest
the way with opery music. The first time you don't like it;
then you get another taste, and it's better; then you go a little
further, and it's first-rate. There's nothing like eddication.
Natur is well enough in her place, but eddication does the job."

Mr. Slow looked grave as he uttered this oracular wisdom, and
his auditors admired.

PHLEBOTOMY A DISEASE.

"Do you think people are troubled as much with fleabottomry
now, doctor, as they used to be before they diskivered the anti-
bug bedstead?" asked Mrs. Partington of the doctor of the old
school who attended upon the family where she was staying.

"Phlebotomy, madam," said the doctor gravely, "is a remedy,
not a disease."

"Well, well," replied she, "no wonder one gets 'em mixed up,
there is so many of 'em. We never heard in old times of tonsors
in the throat, or embargoes in the head, or neurology all over us,
or consternation in the bowels, as we do now-a-days. But it's an
ill wind that don't blow nobody no good, and the doctors flourish
on it like a green baize tree. But, of course, they don't have
anything to do with it,—they can't make them come or go."

The doctor stepped out with a genteel bow, and the old lady
watched him till his cabriolet had turned the corner, her mind
revolving the intricate subject of cause and effect

HIRSUTE ORNAMENTS.

"WELL!" said Mrs. Partington, as she leaned forward, with her hands resting on the window ledge, and peered out into the street through a chink in the blinds. It wasn't a *deep* well, expressive of content or satisfaction, but it was an ejaculatory well, that found expression at some object which she had witnessed in the street. "Well," said she, "I hope that man is married, I declare I do; because, if he isn't, I'm sure he never will be, for a dreadfuler looking creature I never did see, with them mustychokes on his mouth—nobody would'nt have him. I've heard 'em say that Heaven's best gift to man was woman; I should say that the next best gift was a razor to such a man as that. Folks didn't take pride in looking bad in old times!"

She turned thoughtfully to the wall, where hung in military rigidity that profile, the cherished gem of bygone art, the counterfeit presentment of manly grace.

"Ah, Paul!" sighed the dame, "you was an ornament of your specie, and the cheapest among ten thousand, or *more!*" She emphasized the "more," as if the contrast was very great, indeed, between Paul and him who had passed. But the profile took no notice of what she said; its gaze, chained to perpetual straightforwardness, looked never to the right or left; though, at times, she said it bore a kinder expression about the mouth. But this must have been her fancy, which gave to every object she looked upon the hues of her own benignity.

MRS. PARTINGTON AND PROBATE.

"O, WHAT trials a poor widow has to go through!" sighed Mrs. Partington, rocking herself in a melancholy way, and holding the morsel of maccaboy untasted between her thumb and finger; "terrible trials; and, O, what a hardship it is to be executioner to an intestine estate—where enviable people are trying every way to overcome the widow's might; where it's probe it, probe it, probe it, all the time; and the more you probe it the worse it seems! The poor widow never gets justice, for if she gets all, she don't get half enough. I have had one trial of it, and if ever I should marry again, if it should so please Providence to order it, I'll make my husband fabricate his will before he orders his wedding-cake. I'll take Time by the foretop, as Solomon says, you may depend upon it."

She here revived a little, and the subtle powder passed to its destination, and reported itself home by an emphatic sneeze.

EXTRACT from a great unwritten poem of 1051 verses, entitled "Ye Constabel":—

> "Ye constabel from one man took
> A large and ample fee,
> I'll now take one from ye t'other side,
> Said ye constabel, said he."

DOMESTIC PURITY IMPUGNED.

"HAVE you got any rooms to let here, marm?" said a little man to Mrs. Partington, who occupied half of a house, the other half of which was to let, and to whom was entrusted the care of answering the door-bell.

The rooms were shown.

"They are not large," said the little man, deprecatingly.

"No, sir," replied she, "they are not very ruminous; but here are two little bed-rooms contagious that perhaps you didn't see."

He looked in, and, in a supercilious tone, muttered, "*Bugs!*" implying want of cleanliness,—a reflection on the purity of the premises in her charge!

There is a point, as she says, where patience ceases to be virtuous, and she had found it. Indignation choked her utterance; and the little man fortunately departed before it found vent. It was great, the way in which she slammed the door to after him, and ejaculated "*Bugs!*" till the empty rooms in echoing it seemed full of *bugs*. It was a sublime and moral spectacle.

"FARE, MA'AM."

"How do you do, dear?" said Mrs. Partington, smilingly, shaking hands with Burbank, in the Dock-square omnibus, as he held out his five dexter digits towards her.

"Fare, ma'am!" said he, in reply to her inquiry.

"Well, I'm shore, I'm glad of it, and how are the folks at home?"

"Fare, ma'am!" continued he, still extending his hand. The passengers were interested.

"How do you like Boston?" screamed she, as the omnibus rattled over the stones.

"Fare, ma'am!" shouted he, without drawing back his hand; "I want you to pay me for your ride!"

"O!" murmured she, "I thought it was some one that knowed me," and rummaged down in the bottom of her reticule, for a ticket, finding at last five copper cents tied up in the corner of her handkerchief—the "last war" handkerchief, with the stars and stripes involved in it, and the action of the Constitution and Guerriere stamped upon it. But the smile she had given him at first was not withdrawn—there was no allowance made for mistakes at that counter—and she went out, with a lighter heart and a heavier pocket, to catch t'other coach.

PAYING PROMPTLY.

"If there is any place in this world where I like to ransack business more than another," said Mrs. Partington, with animation, untying from the corner of her handkerchief a sum of money she had just received, "if there's any place better than another, it's a bank. There's no dillydalliance, and beating down, and bothering you with a thousand questions, till you don't know whether your heels are up or your head is down; all you have to do is to put your bill on the counter, and they pay it without saying a word."

The old lady had presented a check for a quarter's pension-money, received on account of Paul, who, in the "last war," served a fortnight in fortifying Boston harbour, and got mortar in his eyes, which hurt his "visionary organs," so that he took to glasses.

"MEMENTO MORY."

BEFORE old Roger left boarding at No. 47, he forfeited all regard of the quiet inmates of the house by the perpetration of the following atrocity, which was the true reason of his leaving, and not the quality of the bread-pudding, as many believed. Mory, the Kilby-street clerk, got married, and moved off. It had always been a custom with Mory to pile his dishes up in a curious manner, after he had used them,—cups, saucers, plates, in a heterogeneous heap. A day or two after his departure from the house, old Roger was observed piling his cup and saucer and plates in the same manner, and he took those of his neighbour to add to the pile. The boarders watched him silently, in much surprise, and one of them, a little bolder than the rest, ventured to ask him what he was doing that for.

"O," said Roger, placidly, crowning the pile he had made with the cover of the sugar-bowl, "I am only erecting a memento Mory."

Mr. Blifkins, the serious man, exhorted the more volatile boarders on the impropriety of laughing at such an outrageously sacrilegious use of a respectable dead language. From that day Roger had cold shoulder for dinner, and the coldness of the landlady became suddenly manifest in cold potatoes, and in the rheumatic condition of his room attic; so he left.

OLD BULL'S CONCERT.

"OLD Bull's concert!" said Mrs. Partington, glancing up from her knitting as she read the announcement of the grand concert on Saturday evening, and she smiled as the ridiculous fancy ran through her mind, like a grasshopper in a stubble field, of an old bull giving a concert. "And yet, it isn't so very wonderful," continued she, "for I remember a cat and canary that lived together, and one or t'other of 'em used to sing beautifully. But I wonder what he plays on."

Ike suggested that he played on one of his own horns, which seemed to be reasonable.

"I am glad he is going to give his concert, because, when I went down to hear a great artisan play on a violence, as they called it, though I found out afterwards it was nothing but a fiddle, they were going to charge a florin, till I told 'em I was one of the connections of the Post, and they let me in. I can't think what music an old bull can make, I'm sure. It must be very uproarious, I should think, and better fitted for overturns than for pastureal music."

She closed her critique with a pinch of snuff, and got on to her wires again like a telegraphic despatch, and went ahead, while Ike amused himself by scratching his name with a board nail, in magnificent Roman capitals, upon the newly-painted panel of the kitchen door.

ANGULAR SAXONS.

"I DON'T know," said Mrs. Partington, and the expression, considered as a mere abstraction, was true, for there are some that have more of the world's wisdom and a better knowledge of grammar than the dame; for the school for her teaching was not one of letters. But let us hear her. "I don't know," said she, "about these Angular Saxons being any better than our old-fashioned ones."

Ike had been reading to her an article upon the destiny of the Anglo-Saxon race.

"And as for the race, Isaac," and her voice fell to a pitch of deep solemnity as she spoke, "it isn't proper at all; for when a funeral goes too quick—to say nothing about racing—it always is a forerunner, sometimes, that somebody 'll die before the year's out. The old Saxons were full fast enough, naturally; and after the parish gin out Saxon the surfeit of plate for his officious services, it spruced him right up, and it seemed as if it would have pleased him to bury all of 'em, he was so grateful. No, no, we don't want any Angular Saxons, Isaac, when our own are full good enough."

Ike, as she was talking, had amused himself with tying the old lady's snuff-box in the corner of his handkerchief, and was experimentally swinging it around his head; and she ceased just as the box, released from the knot, flashed against the opposite side, scattering the pungent powder in plenteous profusion upon the sanded floor. Of course he didn't mean to do it, and that was all that saved him.

MRS. PARTINGTON AT THE OPERA.

We were surprised, at the opera, last evening, by having a hand placed upon our shoulder. It was a gentle touch; altogether unlike certain other touches on the shoulder that delinquent men so much dread. It came at a time when we were all absorbed by the melody of the charming Sontag, and were provoked at the intrusion.

"Will you be kind enough to lend me your observatory?" asked a voice we thought we remembered.

Looking round, "Great heavens!" we cried, "Mrs Partington!"

It was, indeed, that estimable dame, but yet it was not; for the black bonnet had disappeared, and a new rigolette adorned her venerable poll, beneath which every sprig of wavy gray was securely tacked. But the smile was there, as warm as a June morning at nine o'clock. She repeated the request to use the pearl and diamond-studded opera-glass, that we had hired at Fetridge's for five shillings,—denominating it an "observatory."

"Is this the right pocus?" said she; "I s'pose I shall have to digest it to my sight, for my poor visionary orgies are giving out."

She levelled both barrels at the singers at once, and brought them down to her, and Pozzolini directed three successive appeals to her tenderness.

"It a'n't no use," said she, as she handed the glass; "I can't understand better with that,—I should have bought one of the lab'ratories at the door."

She beat time gracefully to the music for a while upon the cover of her snuff-box, and then went out, like an exhausted candle, to try and light on Ike, who was trading for a jack-knife with another boy on the gallery stairs.

A SLIGHT MISAPPREHENSION.

MRS. PARTINGTON was at Thackeray's last lecture,—Mr. T. had kindly sent her a card, admitting one,—and, forgetting the theme of the lecture, she leaned over the seat and asked the gentleman before her what the subject was.

"Goldsmith and Sterne, mem," was the reply; "but he is on Sterne, first."

Mrs. Partington blushed. There was evidently a question agitating her mind as to whether she should tarry and hear a lecture from a person so ridiculously postured as Mr. T. must appear. She looked around, meditating a retreat; but the avenue to escape was blocked up, and she thought she might as well stay it out. She watched tremblingly for Mr. Thackeray, and was much relieved by seeing him standing perpendicularly before her. She thought she must have mistaken the meaning of her informant.

APOLLYON BONYPART.

"WHEN will the world get rid of this Apollyon Bonypart?" said Mrs. Partington, as Ike threw down the paper in which he had read a comparison between the "18th Brumaire" and the "coup d'état." In the uncertain glimmerings of her memory, she confounded the nephew and uncle, and her thought took the course the dim reminiscence pointed.

"Apollyon Bonypart! I remember all about him, and his

eighteenth blue mare too. I always wondered where he got so many of 'em,—something like the woolly horse, I guess,—and when he was transplanted to Saint Domingo, Isaac, folks went up to the King's Chapel to sing tedium about it, because they were glad of it. And now he's come back agin, with all his blue mares with him."

The dropping of a stitch brought her down from the new hobby she was riding so furiously, and Ike drew a picture of a blue mare, in chalk, upon the newly-washed kitchen floor.

PAUL AND POLITICS.

" Was Paul inclined to politics?" we asked of Mrs. Partington, as we saw the old dame reading a "grand rally" hand-bill at the corner of the grocery store. She asked us to wait a moment till she " digested" her specs. " Inclined to politics!" said she, and her eyes rested upon the period at the end of the last line, till she seemed to be meditating a full stop. " He was; but he wasn't a propergander, nor an oilygarchist, or an avaritionist, nor a demigod, as some of 'em are; all he wanted was an exercise of his sufferings and the use of his elective French eyes, as he used to say. Ah, Heaven rest him!" exclaimed she, as her eyes rose from the period at the bottom of the bill and rested on the top of the fence. " But did he never get an office, Mrs. P.?" we asked. " Yes," replied she, and we fancied the tone of her voice had an expression of triumph in it— enough to be perceptible, like three drops of paregoric in a teaspoonful of water—" yes, he was put one year for a hogreefer, and got neglected." As we were about asking her opinion of the new constitution, Ike came along whistling " Jordan" and swinging a pint of milk, in a tin pail, around his head, and the old lady forgot her politics in her solicitude about Ike's soiling his new cap.

TROUSSEAU OF PRINCESS WASA.

Ike read, " At Paris, the dressmakers, jewellers, and milliners have all been occupied in furnishing the trousseau of the Princess Wasa."

" Stop, Isaac," said Mrs. Partington, raising her finger, and glancing at him over the top of her spectacles; " is that so?"

He assured her that it was.

G

"Well," continued she, and a blush of offended modesty crossed her features, like the sun-flush on the newly reddened barn-door; "that may be the way they do things in Paris, but it isn't modest to begin with. A woman has no right to wear 'em. 'T is agin natur and decency. And what does she want so many of 'em for? She can't wear but one pair to a time, and here she has got all of the dressmakers making trousers for her, as if she was going to live long enough to wear 'em out. Ah, women a'nt what they were once!"

She rose suddenly as she spoke, and Ike, who was upon the back of her chair, endeavouring to tie a string to a nail in the big beam that traversed the ceiling, was thrown violently against the table, breaking three plates and a teacup in his descent.

PHILOSOPHY OF COUNTRY HEALTH.

"People may say what they will about country air being so good for 'em," said Mrs. Partington, "and how they fat up on it; for my part, I shall always think it is owin' to the vittles. Air may do for camamiles and other reptiles that live on it, but I know that men must have something substanialler."

The old lady was resolute in this opinion, conflict as it might with general notions. She is set in her opinions, very, and in their expression nowise backward.

"It may be as Solomon says," said she; "but I lived at the pasturage in a country town all one summer, and I never heerd a turtle singing in the branches. I say I never heerd it; but it may be so, too, for I have seen 'em in brooks under the trees, where they perhaps dropped off. I wish some of our great naturals would look into it."

With this wish for light, the old lady lighted her candle and went to bed.

THE PROMENADE.

We sat directly in front of Mrs. Partington at Jullien's concert, one night, and were pleased to witness the marked attention that she paid to the performance. The first part had been concluded, and the "fifteen minutes' intermission for promenade," announced on the bill, had been well spent, when we felt a finger laid upon the arm that rested upon the back of the next seat, and a whispered voice was breathed into our sinister ear:

"When is he going to carry it round?"

We looked at her inquiringly, and she looked inquiringly back again.

"Carry it round?"

"Yes," replied she, "the promenade here. 'T is the refreshment part of the entertainment, isn't it?"

We explained to her the meaning of the word "promenade," and, with a long-drawn "O!" like an extended cipher, she sank back into her seat. Ike was blowing peas at a gentleman's boot projecting through the lattice work of the gallery.

MRS. PARTINGTON IN THE CROWD.

"Don't go anigh it, Isaac," said Mrs. Partington, with nervous anxiety, on the day of the great railroad jubilee procession, as the carriage, bearing the big gun, came by where she and Ike were standing. She had been very nervous all the morning, and had made some curious mistakes. When the procession first came along, she waved her handkerchief at an alderman, taking him to be the president; and Marshal Tukey she thought was Lord Elgin.

"Don't go anigh it,—it's one of the pesky Paxon guns we read of; they call 'em peace-makers, because they tear people all to pieces; and, depend upon it, Isaac, if a man got hit once or twice with such a gun as that, my idea is, that there wouldn't be much left of him. O, the wickedness of men, that they should learn war, and kill people, and spoil good clothes, and act more like Kottenpots or salvages than they do like men! They say this Mr. Paxton has got up a Christian Parish in London, and everybody is going to see it. Well, I hope he will tend it himself, and get good, and repent of the evil he has done. But, I'm sure, I hope he won't have any such machines as that, ever, to help his preaching."

The noise of the passing crowd drowned half her remarks, and, at that moment, a marshal backed his horse near where she and Ike stood, with a command to her to "stand back." It was astonishing how the flies, or something, troubled that marshal's horse all the while he stood there.

ANCIENT AND MODERN REMEDIES CONTRASTED.

"They don't doctor folks now as my physician learnt me," said Mrs. Partington, sagely tapping her snuff-box by the cov-

of a friend lying indisposed. Her gesture was very expressive, and the profundity of a whole Med. Fac. beamed from her spectacles. She took a pinch of Farwell's subtle maccaboy in her fingers, and shut the box, and laid it away in her capacious pocket; then, with her closed forefinger and thumb raised, went on with her remarks,—"They don't subscribe for folks now as they used to. My doctor used to tell me,—and he never lost any of his patience but once, and that was an old man of ninety-seven, whose days were shortened because he hadn't strength to swallow, —he used to tell me,—and I've been with him thousands of times with sick folks,—he used to tell me, first, said he, give 'em apecae, to clear the stomach; then give 'em purgatory to clear the bowels; then put a blister on the neck if the head aches; and have 'em blooded if there is a tenderness of the blood to the head; and put hot poultices on to the feet, arter soaking 'em in hot water. There wan't none of your Homerpathics, nor Hydrapathics, nor no other pathics then, and what was done might be sure it would either kill or cure!"

She inhaled the dust with great unction, and the patient, who lay making squares and diamonds out of the roses on the roompaper, took courage, because he had fallen upon times of more physical mildness.

MR. SLOW IN THE MOON.

Mr. Slow and Abimelech were out looking upon the moon, as it gleamed above them in the sky. The moon, as they gazed, passed behind a dark cloud, the edge of which gleamed like silver.

" How beautiful! " said Abimelech.

" Yes, my son," said Mr. Slow, solemnly, " that 'ere's well got up. Some people say they have brighter moons in other places than our'n, but I say that's all moonshine. Look at it, 'Bimelech, as it hangs up there now, as bright as a dollar, and don't you believe any of the gammoning stories about its being a green cheese."

" But, father," asked Abimelech, his son, " isn't the story true about the man in the moon ?"

" Certinly, my son, certinly," said Mr Slow, looking down at him; " that's all true, that is, 'cause it's in the primer."

Abimelech was satisfied—so was Mr. Slow.

MRS. PARTINGTON ON REMEDIES.

"THIS is an age of enervation in medicine, sure enough!" said Mrs. Partington, as she glanced at the column of new and remarkable specifics; "why will people run after metaphysics and them nostrums, when, by taking some simple purgatory, they can get well so soon? It's all nonsense, it is; and if people, instead of dosing themselves with calumny and bitters, would only take exercise and air a little more, and wash themselves with care and a crash towel, they would be all the better for it."

She said this on her own experience. As for "diet drink," and summer beverages, Mrs. P. is very noted.

A NEW INSTRUMENT.

"WHEN is he going to bring on the *wioleen ?*" whispered Mrs. Partington to a neighbour, at the Melodeon, after listening through the first part of Ole Bull's concert.

"That's it, ma'am, which he is now playing on."

"Why, that's a fiddle, a'n't it! Good gracious! why can't they call things by their right names?"

And she left the hall, saying to the door-keeper, as she passed, that it was only a *fiddle* after all.

BLEAK HOUSE.

"DICKENS is fast getting along to the denouncement of the Bleak House," said Mrs. Partington, as she saw a paragraph mentioning the approaching denouement of the story. "Well, I should think he would have denounced it long ago, and had it prepared, for I don't believe they could have made him pay one mill of rent, unless he did it at his own auction. Bleak House, indeed; and Mr. Dickson a poor man, too, with aliments enough on him to patternise a whole hospital himself!"

The picture of the Good Samaritan handing the wounded Jew a quart bottle of Sarsaparilla Bitters attracted her attention, and she delivered Ike a private lecture on the humanities, while he sat pulling the cat's tail in the dark side of the chimney-corner.

ADMIRATION FOR ELOQUENCE.

"DEAR me, how fluidly he does talk!" said Mrs. Partington, recently, at a temperance lecture. "I am always rejoiced when he mounts the nostril, for his eloquence warms me in every nerve and cartridge of my body. Verdigrease itself could'nt be more smooth than his blessed tongue is;" and she wiped her spectacles with her cotton bandanna, and never took her eyes from the speaker during the whole hour he was on the stand.

NAVES OF THE CRYSTAL PALACE.

"WELL," said Mrs. Partington, as Ike read the paragraph from the *Post*, that the decorators were at work on the two naves of the Crystal Palace. She paused at the "well" before she went further into it, and Ike stopped reading to hear what she had to say, and chewed up a part of the paper into spit-balls, which he amused himself with by throwing at the old white-pine dresser in the corner. "Well," said she,—this is the same *well* we left some time since,—"I am glad they are taking time by the fire lock, and looking arter the knaves aforehand. Knaves in the Christian parish, indeed! But they will get in, the best that can be done. There's many a one, I dessay, in all parishes that has a sanctuary in his face, but with the cloak of hypocrisy in his heart. Read on, Isaac."

And the old lady looked up at the black-framed ancient picture of Susannah and the elders, and patted her box reflectively.

MR. BISBEE'S CONFESSION.

IT was a rash promise that I, Jeremiah Bisbee, had made to the youngest Miss Teel to gallant her to church. I knew that she would be offended if I did not comply, and yet how I felt! The previous evening's amusement had extended well towards daylight, and a more miserably-feeling fellow than myself never did rouse himself at the sound of breakfast-bell on a Sunday morning. But the promise was made, and the glory of a new pair of plaid pants and a red velvet vest was to blaze beside the modest beauty of Miss Seraphima in the Rev. Mr. Blunt's church.

I had no seat there, but my cousins, the Misses Titmarsh,

who owned a pew in the broad aisle, had many times invited me
to sit with them, informing me that there was plenty of room,
and I determined to avail myself of their invitation. I had heard
them describe, too, the occupants of adjacent pews, and had been
given to understand that the Ogglers and Spighs, the aforesaid
occupants, were the most respectable people in town, and that
they felt rather envious at the superior position of "our"
pew; for so the *young* ladies (forty-seven if they were a day)
called it.

The day was bright, the pants fitted to a charm, the red vest
gleamed in the sun, my coat was neatly brushed, and, with an
unexceptional hat, and a pair of brilliant boots, I felt myself to
be "some." The sleepy feeling with which the morning commenced, was overcome by the momentary excitement of walking
and talking with a charming girl; a triumph over Somnus that
I thought truly wonderful.

We reached the church,—a large, venerable, sleepy pile, having
a good many pews in it; the latter, a characteristic, I believe, of
churches generally.

As ill luck would have it, we had a very dull preacher,—a
duller I never knew,—trite and common-place, without originality or fervour, and insufferably long. I felt sleepy at the pro-
pounding of the text, which was, as near as I remember, "Sleep
on, and take your rest;" and every wakeful feeling within me
began to grow heavy about the eyes at the injunction. I struggled against slumber, as a man overboard would struggle with
the tide. My eyelids dropped in spite of me, and when I would
open them, they felt as if they were interlaced with sticks, and
my sleepy soul seemed looking through a grating of wicker work.
The eyes of my cousins, the Misses Titmarsh, were wide open
upon me, the bright eyes of Seraphima were upon me, the eyes
of the Ogglers and Spighs were upon me, for the Misses Titmarsh had informed me, in a whisper, that they were here in
full force, and that the new plaid pants, and the red vest, and
Seraphima's new bonnet,—a charming thing, by the way,—would
produce a tremendous envy among their opponents in the adjacent pew.

In my sleepy reflections I saw the utter disgrace that would
attend upon my cousins, the Titmarshes, if I misbehaved. I
thought upon them, positively, more than upon my own shame.
I thought of the horror they would feel were I to speak aloud, or
laugh, or tumble down, or commit any extravagance in a dream.
All of the tricks I had ever practised in my sleep came up before
me, frightfully magnified. What if I should practise some

them over again, or get up on the backs of the pews and go round, as Amina foots it over the tiles, in the opera?

I struggled manfully with sleep, but I found I couldn't hold out long. Hum-m-m, hummed on that long sermon!—Upon my honour, I don't believe I heard a word of it besides the text, unless it were the word "sleep," which seemed profusely scattered, like poppies, along the tedious way. I found myself rapidly sinking. The faces by which I was surrounded were melting away, the Ogglers and the Spighs were becoming oblivious, and the preacher, just taking the form of a huge black beetle impaled on a pin, was humming a dull drone on one continuous key, when, mustering resolution, I roused myself, thrust my hand hastily into my pocket to pull out my handkerchief, when, —the Ogglers and Spighs were all looking, and so were the Misses Titmarsh and Seraphima,—when,—I blush to say it, though it was the means of my becoming a reformed man, and a tolerable member of society, and the father of a large family,— when I pulled my handkerchief out, *a pack of cards*, a deposit of the previous night, came leaping out with it, and, as if actuated by the devil who invented them, they darted about in almost as many directions as there were cards, brazenly showing themselves in the holy house, to my utter confusion of face.

Had my worst enemy seen me then, he must have pitied me. I was wide awake now. The concentrated redness of every red card was painted upon my face, and the blackness of every black one was transferred to my heart. The spots on the cards, to my heated fancy, seemed bigger than a cart-wheel. I heard a suppressed titter among the Ogglers and the Spighs. Just then the eldest Miss Titmarsh fainted. "Heaven be thanked for this!" says I; "here's an opening;" and, seizing the unconscious spinster, I made for the door as speedily as possible. Placing her in charge of the sexton, I ran with all haste for the doctor. Strange that those medical gentlemen should be away at such a time! I left an urgent order on the slates of six of them, and was told that five of the six, an hour afterwards, met in consultation on the steps of Rev. Mr. Blunt's church.

As I said before, I have now reformed, and sit just in the shadow of life's afternoon, looking back over the events of its morning, rejoicing with hopeful trust, that the errors of youth may not be carried forward to the account of mature age, if repentance make atonement for the past. The Misses Titmarsh forgave me, and Seraphima, in a long life of devoted attention on my part, has quite forgot that Sunday's mortification.

GERMANIA BAND.

"How do you like the music, Mrs. P.?" asked her neighbour of the old lady as she stood listening to the Germania band, one evening on the common, and beating time on the cover of her snuff-box.

"Beautiful!" replied she, enraptured, "oncommon beautiful! It seems almost like the music of the syrups. I think the Geranium band the sweetest of any of 'em. Can you tell me," said she, in a big whisper, "which is Mr. Bergamot?"

The name of Bergamot was associated with her rappee, and hence her solicitude.

She was told that Mr. Bergman belonged to the Germania Society, and that the leader of the Germania Serenaders was Mr. Schnapp.

A smile lit up her face, revealed in the declining twilight, as she asked if he was akin to Mr. Aromatic Schnapps, the gentleman that imported so much gin. Her ear was arrested by the strains of the music, and the black bonnet waved in unison with a waltzing measure, as Isaac sat upon the grass in contemplation of a dog's tail before him, wondering what the effect would be if he should stick a pin in it.

THE SIAMESE TWINS.

Messrs. Chang and Eng—those interesting exotics, from whose land all the golden fountains and talking lauras, and singing trees that graced our juvenile literature were derived—were much gratified by an introduction to Mrs. Partington, one of whom assured her, that he had heard of her in Siam many years ago, but the other didn't recollect about it. On informing her of their intention to go to Saratoga or Newport the coming summer, the old dame wondered at the determination.

"How crowded you will be!" said she, "accommodations are so scarce; though, I dare say, you could, upon a 'mergency, both sleep in one bed."

The suggestion was a happy one—all the difficulty was removed in an instant—and the dual gentleman smiled a thankee with his four lips, and Mrs. Partington waved a parting benediction to him with her green cotton umbrella, as he disappeared in the crowd.

CATCHING AN OMNIBUS.

"IF you want to take a 'bus," said Mr. Sphynx, in his oracular manner, "you must be 'mazing sly ; you musn't go boldly up to 'em, 'cause they'll certingly be full,—room for twelve, and seventeen inside,—or the driver won't see you, if you shake your umbrel or cane at him, never so much. 'Buses are queer critters— very queer ; it takes sunthing of a man to understand their natur. When you want one, there a'n't one coming. Put your head out in the rain, and look every which way, you can't see hide nor hair of one. Wait till the next one comes—that's full ; so's the next. Then you get a little miff'd, and says you, ' I'll walk ! ' Start in the rain—get wet ; when you get almost where you want to go, 'long comes one of 'em, like blazes—lots of room—looking at you as much as to say, ' See here, old boy ! don't you wish you'd ha' waited ?' and whisks by like a racer. If you see a 'bus a little ways ahead, and run yourself into a fever to catch it, two to one it'll be the wrong 'bus, and you'll have to walk, arter all. Now the way to do is this :—Act jest as if you don't care a snap whether you ride or not. Be indifferent, and one'll come right along ; don't be uneasy 'bout getting a seat, and there'll be plenty of room ; conclude that you'll walk, and you may have a whole 'bus to yourself. That's the way to come it over 'em !" Saying which, and shaking his head profoundly, Mr. Sphynx retired.

MYSTERIOUS ACTION OF RATS.

" As for the rats," said Mrs. Partington, as she missed several slices of cake, the disappearance of which she imputed to them, "it a'n't no use to try to get rid of 'em. They rather like the vermin anecdote, and even chlorosive supplement they don't make up a face at. It must be the rats," continued she, thoughtfully, and took a large thumb and forefinger full of rappee to help her deliberation,—"it can't be Isaac that took the cake, because he is a perfect prodigal of virtue, and wouldn't deceive me so, for, I might leave a house full of bread with him and he wouldn't touch it."

Ike sat there demurely, with his right foot upon his left knee, thinking what a capital sunglass one eye of the old lady's specs would make, while a trace of crumbs was visible about his mouth. It is feared that not even chlorosive supplement, nor anything weaker than a padlock, will save Mrs. Partington's cake.

MRS. P. ON THE MISSISSIPPI.

"WHEN will the Father of Waters come along ?" asked Mrs. Partington, as she sat looking at a panorama of the Mississippi, in the last hours of its exhibition.

"The Father of Waters !" replied the individual addressed, "why, this is it that you are seeing before you."

"Goodness me! is it?" said she. "Why, I've digested my specs to look arter a big man with the dropsy, and it's nothing but a river, arter all. How I wish they'd call things by their proper names !"

There was something of disappointment in her tone ; but when afterwards she remarked to herself, "I wonder if that water will wash?" it was a beautiful tribute from Benevolence to Genius.

"ENTERED at the Custom House ?" said Mrs. Partington, pondering on the expression ; "I don't see how the vessels ever got in; but I am glad that the collector cleared 'em right out again. It will learn them better manners next time, I think."

PROVISIONS OF THE CONSTITUTION.

"PROVISIONS of the Constitution !" said Mrs. Partington, with an earnest air and tone ; "for my part I should be glad to see 'em. Heaven and all of us knows provisions is scarce enough and dear enough, and if they can turn the Constitution to so good a use I'm glad of it. Anything that will have a tenderness to cheapen the necessities of life,"—and here she laid her finger on the cover of her box, and looked earnestly at a cracked sugar-bowl in the "buffet" in the corner, containing the onion-seeds, and the bone-buttons, and the scarlet beans, and the pieces of twine, long-gathered from accumulative paper-tea-bags,—"I am agreeable to it, and if they can turn the Constitution and all the ships of war to carrying provisions, I am shore they will do more good then they do now, a good many of 'em."

She here ran down like an eight-day clock, and she smiled as Ike rushed in with his arms full of votes, and his face full of fun and molasses candy, and asked her if he shouldn't give her a "tig wicket."

SEVERE, BUT JUST.

"DOLLY PRIM a spinster, indeed!" said Mrs. Partington, as she heard her unmarried neighbour in the back parlour termed thus. "I should like to know what upon airth she spins but street-yarn; for she's gadding from morning to night. The wheel she spins on would be harder to find, a great deal, than the fifth wheel of a coach!"

O! she could be severe, could Mrs. Partington; but there was generally a commingling of the bitter and sweet, the wormwood and molasses, in her rebukes, that tempered acidity, and made reproof wholesome.

MRS. PARTINGTON AND PIETY.

DEACON SNARL, in exhortation, would often allude to the "place where prayer is 'wonted' to be made."

"Ah!" said Mrs. Partington to herself, "there's nothing like humility in a Christian. I'm glad you confess it. I don't know a place under the canister of heaven where prayer is wanted more to be made than here, and I hope you'll be forgiven for the rancorous butter you sold me yesterday."

She was a simple-minded woman, was Mrs. P., and was apt to get the world mixed up with her devotion; believing, somehow, that Christian duty prescribed worldly justice. She had not been long a member.

MEDALLIC PROSPECTS.

"I DON'T see," said Mrs. Partington, as Ike came home from the examination, and threw his books into one chair, and his jacket in another, and his cap on the floor, saying that he didn't get the medal,—"I don't see why you didn't get the medal, for, certainly, a more meddlesome boy I never knew. But never mind, dear; when the time comes round again you'll get it."

What hope there was in her remark for him! and he took courage and one of the old lady's doughnuts, and sat wiping his feet on a clean stocking, that the dame was preparing to darn, that lay by her side.

MRS. PARTINGTON BEATING UP.

"THERE's poor Hardy Lee called again," said Mrs. Partington on a trip from Cape Cod to Boston. The wind was a-head, and the vessel had to beat up, and the order to put the helm "hard a lee" had been heard through the night. "Hardy Lee, again! I declare I should think the poor creetur would be completely exasperated with fatigue; and I'm certain he hasn't eat a blessed mouthful of anything all the while. Captain, do call the poor cretur down, or Natur can't stand it."

There was a tremour in her voice as indignant humanity found utterance. "It a'n't Christian—it's more like the treatment of Hottenpots or heathen!"

The captain went on deck, and a sudden lurch of the vessel sent the old lady on her beam-ends among some boxes, recovering from which forgetfulness of "Hardy Lee" ensued, and this tack brought her to the wharf.

A DEAD SHOT.

"How do you feel with such a shocking-looking coat on?" said a young clerk, of more pretension than brains, one morning.

"I feel," said old Roger, looking at him steadily, with one eye half-closed, as if taking aim at his victim, "I feel, young man, as if I had a coat on which has been paid for,—a luxury of feeling which I think you will never experience;" and then he quietly resumed the reading of the *Post*, and the young clerk made no further remark on the subject.

SHOCKING JOKE.

"I SEE," said old Roger to a farmer topping corn, "that to one branch of your industry you are its worst enemy."

"Why?" asked the farmer.

"Because," replied he, "you are always raising shocks for the corn-market."

"Yes," quietly replied the farmer, "but the market is always saying, 'lend us your ears.'"

Old Roger and the farmer smiled at each other as they parted.

MRS. PARTINGTON LOOKING OUT.

"I can't make it out," said Mrs. Partington one morning, when she first moved to the city, after the railroad ploughshare had upturned her hearth-stone. "I can't make it out;" and she reached further out of the window, to the imminent danger of the "embargo" returning again to her head, or of a somerset into the street below. She had caught the sound, "Here's haddick!" from stentorian lungs under her window, and she could not make out what the sounds meant.

"I wish I knowed what the poor critter was crying about, but I thought he said he had a sick headache; and I declare I pity the poor soul that has got such a distressing melody as that."

She drew in her head, like a clam, and shut down the window, to shut out the sounds of a misery she could not relieve.

FORESEEING THINGS BEFOREHAND.

"I wonder who is coming here to-day?" said Mrs. Partington, at the breakfast table, turning her cup and working the tea-grounds to their oracular position. A procession was advertised to pass her door. "I wonder who is coming here to-day? Here's a horse, and a wheelbarrow, and a tub; and there's a big G and a cipher; and here's a flock of geese and a cow. The cow and the geese must mean the procession, that's clear; but what can the big G stand for, and the rest of 'em? It must mean our seventh cousin, Mrs. Tubbs; and it is so kind of her to remember her poor relations at such times, as she always does. Yes, it must be her, 'cause there's a tub, and the wheelbarrow must run for an omnibus; but what can the cipher be? I guess, though, that don't mean anything. Scour up the German silver spoons, Margaret; we must be hospitable. I dare say she would be to us if she should ever ask us, and we should go."

The prediction was fulfilled, and the fat lady occupied the front seat in Mrs. Partington's private box.

A SINUOSITY.

OLD ROGER was seated at the dinner-table by the side of Sera-phima, the youngest of the five marriageable daughters. The conversation turned upon conundrums and queer comparisons. The old fellow leaned back in his chair, and, wiping the traces of soup from his mouth, said, as he took the young lady's hand in his own, " See this fair hand, now, white as a snow-flake, and rich with dimpled beauties!"—Seraphima smiled.—" Who is there among you that can tell me why this sweet hand is like the remains of that 'hock-shin" soup before us all ? "

The hand was drawn back suddenly,—that fair hand, compared with a vile pile of beef sinews! The boarders were astonished at his audaciousness,—Seraphima frowned.

" You can't guess, can you ? " said the jolly old fellow. " Well," continued he, " it is because there is such tendonness in it."

He pronounced it " tenderness," and Seraphima smiled again; but the boarders, who had found the meat rather hard, didn't see the relevancy of it,—they didn't know what *tendon* meant, no more 'n a cow knows about its grandmother.

THE SCIENCE OF FISH.

" I wonder what this '*itch theology*' is," said Mrs. Partington, giving a somewhat novel pronunciation of the old science, as she read the announcement of the lecture by Professor Agassiz; " what in the name of Old Scratch *can* it be? I suppose it must mean the itch for meddling with politics and things that doesn't concern 'em, and running down their own country and relations, and praising up everybody else, and at war with everything, all the time they are preaching peace."

Some one explained that it was the science of fishes.

" Well, well," said the lady, " it's just as well; for a minister preaching politics is like a fish out of water—he is out of his ailment."

She passed over to the deaths and marriages, and Ike ganged his hook, with an afternoon's smelting in his eye, and a ball of Mrs. Partington's piping-cord in his pocket for contingencies.

ETERNAL INDEBTEDNESS.

" When I lent her the eggs," said Mrs. Partington, " she said she would be eternally indebted to me, and I guess she will. How can people do so ? I would go round the world on all-fours a begging, before I would be guilty of such a thing. Ah, well, it takes everybody to make a world ! "

And she put in saleratus enough to make up for the non-returned eggs; her neighbour had decidedly taken a rise out of her.

BORROWING NEWSPAPERS.

"SHALL I have the goodness to look at your newspaper one moment?" asked Mrs. Partington at the grocery shop.

"Certainly, my dear madam, with the greatest reluctance possible," replied the grocer.

They exchanged glances, and there was so much of thankfulness in her eye, that he almost made up his mind to subscribe for another paper for her express accommodation.

PROMISING CHILDREN.

"WHAT a to-do people make because children happen to know something when they are young!" said Mrs. Partington, as she read an account of many men who had been distinguished in early years. "Now, all these together don't know so much, by one-half, as Dolly Sprigg's baby. That *is* a perfect prodigal, to be sure; sich an intellect! Why, it got through its goo-googles, and into its bar-bars, afore it was seven months old; and when it was only a year and a half old it emptied a snuff-box down its precious old grandmother's throat as she was asleep, and came nigh suffocating the old lady afore she could wake up to conscientiousness and spit it out. There never was sich another, its mother says,—and who knows so well as a mother what a child is, that has watched over it, and seen it expand itself like a tansy blossom, and sweet as a young cauliflower?"

The old lady was always eloquent on this topic; she was a believer in prodigies, and thought Solomon must have consulted some young mother when he wrote that "every generation grows wiser and wiser."

FORGIVENESS OF WRONG.

"HE called me a termagrunt, and said I wasn't any better than I should be," said Mrs. Partington, as she threw her shawl into the water-bucket, and her bonnet on the floor, on her return from her landlord's, where she had vainly sought an extension of time for payment of the rent; "there never was such an aspiration cast upon one of our family before; there is no such thing in our whole craniology; and, if there is any statuary or law for slander, I'll see if he can prove it. The termagrunt I don't mind so much; but to be called no better than I should be—the mean, penny-catching curmudgin! But no, it's wrong to call him names; it makes me most as bad as he is; I'll borrow the money and pay him, I will, and shew him that I don't bear mallets;" and she brightened up in the thought of this mode of revenge, bustling about and putting the house to rights in the best humour in the world. Her conduct was a sermon and seven tracts on the principle of forgiveness of wrong.

TAKING PICTURES.

"THAT is a splendid likeness!" exclaimed Augustus, rapturously, as Mrs. Partington showed him a capital daguerreotype of her own venerable frontispiece.

"Isn't it," said she, smiling; "isn't it! Isn't it beautifully done? All the cemetery of the features, and cap-strings, and specs, is brought out as nateral as if from a painter's palate. Any young lady, now," continued she, "who would like to have the liniments of her pretended husband to look at when he is away, could be made happy by this blessed and cheap contrivance of making pictures out of sunshine."

She clasped the cover of the picture, paused as if pursuing in her own mind the train of her admiration, and went out like an exploded rocket.

PRECOCITY.

THE elder Smith was somewhat astonished one evening at finding a berry pie for tea,—a rather remarkable thing in his gastronomical experience, for Mr. Smith indulged in few luxuries, for reasons which will be understood by people of limited means. It was an excellent pie, the *chef d'œuvre* of the culinary skill of Mrs. Smith, who prided herself upon what she could do if she only had the "grediences." Smith, junior, numbering some three summers, sat opposite his sire.

"My son," said the old 'un, during a pause in the work of mastication, "did your mother make this pie to-day?"

"Certainly," said the precocious youth; "she didn't, of course, make it to-morrow!"

The elder Smith looked mournfully at the miniature edition of himself, then, wiping the crumbs from his mouth, and ejaculating "So young!" he left the house.

H

MR. THIMBLE'S MOUSE-TRAP.

THE old gentleman one morning discovered a mouse in his bed-chamber. A mouse or a rat was what he held in the utmost dread, and even the idea of getting his hand on one by any accident, always gave him a tremour. Seeing the little animal thus in his very bed-chamber was most provoking, and, reaching for an oaken cane always at the head of his bed, a defence against hostile invaders of this " inner shrine," he at once vowed the mouse's destruction, and, cane in hand, started upon its accomplishment.

" Ha ! " said he, between his fixed teeth, as he closed the door and firmly grasped his stick ; " now, Mr. Mouse, I've got you— I'll fix your flint for you ! " and the poor little timid thing running into a corner, the old gentleman levelled a furious blow at him, repeating his threat to fix his flint for him.

This offer to fix the flint of the mouse is hardly intelligible in this age of patent matches ; but Mr. Thimble lived in tinder box times, when flint and steel were inseparable, and he probably thought that an animal so inclined to steal must have a flint.

The blow was wrongly directed, and the mouse escaped to another corner.

Another blow, and another, resulted in the same manner, until at last the mouse finding cover beneath an antique bureau, the old gentleman was compelled to exert all his generalship to bring him out.

But in vain he got down on all-fours and looked beneath the bureau ; in vain was the cane thrust in the direction of his eyes ; the enemy was nowhere to be seen, and Mr. T. got up, flushed with the exercise, brushed his knees, and went down to breakfast, wondering where the little animal had gone.

After relating the incident, he was calmly engaged in cooling his coffee, when, dropping his cup, he darted from the table into the middle of the floor, dragged half the breakfast things after him, and practised antics very unbecoming in an elderly gentleman of sixty-two.

His family, astonished to see him thus, had incipient ideas of lunatic asylums and strait jackets dart across their minds—the old gentleman the while capering about the room like a mad dancing-master, shaking his right leg as if St. Vitus had selected this member for his particular favour, regardless of the rest, until, with a tremendous spasmodic kick, out fell the mouse from where he had secreted himself !

It was long before Mr. T. regained composure.

Some time after, speaking of his activity, Mrs. Thimble remarked,—

"My dear, I didn't think it was in you."

Mr. T. looked queerly at her, as she uttered this, but didn't say anything.

MRS. PARTINGTON vs. COOK-BOOKS.

"A BEEFSTEAK fried in water," said Mrs. Partington, "it seems to me, must taste very much as if it was biled. They do have *such* curious idees about cooking now-a-days! And people has to learn lots of outlandish names before they know what they've got for dinner. Ah! the good old times was the best, when people seasoned their dishes with flag-root and such spices, and a poor man's fragile repast was eaten when he knew what he had to be thankful for."

What a cook she is, to be sure! And isn't it the cause of rejoicing for a week among the boys of the neighbourhood when she fries up a batch of doughnuts, and Ike knows where they are kept? No wonder she thought, as she said, that he eat like Pharaoh's lean kind, that eat up the fat of the land of Egypt.

ON ELOCUTION

"O, DOESN'T he disclaim fluidly!" exclaimed Mrs. Partington, delightedly, as she listened to the exercises of the Humtown Intellectual Mutual Improvement Society. Her admiration knew no bounds as a young declaimer, with inspiration truly Demosthenic, launched the flashing beams of his eloquence broadcast among his auditors, with thrilling, dazzling, burning force; anon soaring like a rocket into the "empyrean blue," dashing helter skelter amidst the stars, and harnessing the fiery comets to the car of his genius; anon scouring the land like a racer, the hot sparks, like young lightning, marking his Phaetonish course; anon breaking through the terraqueous shell, and revelling in Hadean horrors in underground localities somewhere.

The voice of Mrs. Partington, whom we left standing on the threshold of her admiration some way back, recalls us to herself.

"How fluidly he talks! He ought to be a minister, I declare; and how well he would look with a surplus on, to be sure! He stands on the nostrum as if he was born and bred an oratorio!"

his life. I wish the President was here to-night; I know he'd see he was an extr'ord'nary young man, and like as not appoint him minister extr'ord'nary, instead of some that never preached any at all."

The old lady beat time with her fan to his gesticulations, nodding the black bonnet approvingly, and smiled as the young man told the world that Franklin had made it a present of the printing-press.

OUTRAGE.

DURING a concert one night, a reckless individual, in the upper gallery of the large hall in which it was held, whose name we did not ascertain, allowed his bill of the concert to slip through his fingers, which, falling below, by the rule of gravitation, fell suddenly upon the exposed head of one of our first young men ! The effect of the concussion upon an object so tender may be well imagined. Smelling-bottles were called for, and, none being at hand, one young lady applied a glove to the sufferer's nose, which, having been lately cleansed with turpentine had the effect of bringing him to. The diabolical perpetrator of the act had the audicity to look over the edge of the gallery and grin at the injury he had done, but, before the officer could get to the gallery and arrest him, he had flown.

P.S.—We wish it to be distinctly understood that it was the *glove*, and not the *nose*, that had been cleaned with the turpentine.

IKE IN THE COUNTRY.

DURING the last winter Ike was sent to visit some of Mrs. Partington's relatives, who live on the borders of the Great Bay. Squid River, which empties into the bay, is a very beautiful stream in summer, but in winter it is dreary enough, with the tall trees, stripped of their foliage, standing, as it were, shivering upon its brink. But it is a rare skating course from Moose village to the river's junction with the bay.

Ike had used up all his resources for fun at the end of the third day. He had snowballed the cattle into a frenzy, caught all the hens in a box trap, tied the pigs together by the legs, sucked all the eggs he could find, and was looking round for something else to do, while the boys were at school. He was just calculating, as he poised a snowball, how near he could come to a tame pigeon on the window-sill without hitting it, when the glass was saved by the appearance of the house-cat outside the sacred precinct of the kitchen.

Ike had watched this cat wistfully ever since he had been there, and the cat had manifested a strange repugnance to him ever since he trod on her tail as she lay by the stove. He immediately seized upon her, and expedients, never wanting, soon suggested themselves to him.

There were plenty of clam-shells about the yard, and, selecting four of the smoothest, he, by the aid of some grafting wax at hand, soon had Tabby beautifully shod with clam-shells and on the way to the river. Ike's idea was to learn her to skate!

The river was smooth as glass, and a sharp wind blew along its surface towards the bay. "Now Puss," said Ike, as he pushed her upon the ice, "go it!" An instinct of danger instantly seized upon her. Her claws, which Ike had found so sharp a short time before, were now useless to her, and, with a growl of spite, she swelled her caudal appendage to an enormous size, which, taking the wind, impelled the poor feline like a clipper over the slippery path. The tail stood straight as a topmast, and grew bigger and bigger, and faster and faster flew the animal to which the tail belonged. Ike laughed till he cried to see the cat scudding before the wind. But now the bay lay before her, and far out over the smooth ice was the blue water of the sea.

The result can be guessed. The cat never came back, and everybody wondered what had become of her, and thought it argued ill luck for a cat to leave a house so suddenly. Ike thought so, especially for the cat.

Ike's conscience reproached him sadly, but he compromised the matter by leaving the tenants of the barnyard in peace all the while he staid there, and came home with a pocket full of doughnuts and an enviable reputation for propriety.

THE NEW YEAR—AN ALLEGORY.

"WHAT are your intentions towards Miss New-Year?" sternly asked the old Guardian of Years, as Time, in the garb of youth, stepped forward to make his proposals. The fair being to whom he aspired, stood veiled before him, in mystical beauty, beside the seer, whose dim eyes had seen the birth and death of thousands of years, and whose beard was white with the frost of centuries, and whose voice creaked with the rust of many ages.

Time, buoyant with the hopes of youth, promised much. Their union, he said, would be fruitful of great events. Joy and prosperity would attend upon it. By their union, the arms of the weak would be strengthened; the tyrant's power be shorn of its might; the poor and down-trodden be exalted; the desponding be made to sing for joy; abuse be banished from the earth; the wrath of man be restrained; and the struggle for right be crowned with success.

The old guardian shook his head incredulously, and a tear fell upon his gray beard as he spoke:

"Alas! alas!" he said, "the same promises were made by your sire to her fair mother, and broken, as have been all the promises of Time since the world began. Where is the fruition of the glorious hopes held out for bygone years? They have found their end in gloom and disappointment. How can I trust, then, this precious charge to your arms in view of olden failures?"

Then young Time, laying down his hour-glass and gaily swinging his scythe among the few weeds left of the herbage of the old year, made answer, with a firm tone and a cheerful air:—

"The violated promises of others should not be the criterion for judging of mine; nor their failure be urged as a presage of my own ill-success. Let me prove myself by my acts, and if endeavour may win the goal, my chance is good. Let me try."

The old guardian grasped Time by the hand approvingly; the hand of the virgin year was placed in his, and, as the clock struck the hour of twelve, the form of the old seer faded from view, and the mystical one, for better and worse, for joy and sorrow, became the wedded bride of Time.

PERSONAL cleanliness is a virtue, but it is not pleasant to see a man cleaning his teeth with a questionable pocket-handkerchief; neither is it to see a man, however attentive he may be to the wants of his family, put a beef-steak in the crown of his hat, and fill his trousers' pockets with cucumbers. It don't look well.

THE ARCHITECTURAL BLACK EYE.

WE met old Guzzle one day, with a terrible black eye. "Ah!" said we to the interesting individual, "bad eye that."

"Yes, that 'ere's a architectural eye."

We asked an explanation.

"I say this 'ere's a architectural eye, because I got it from the Elizabethan architecture of our house."

We were in the dark as much as ever.

"T'other night," continued he, "I went home partially tight. I say partially, for, 'pon my honour, I had drank but seven times during the evening. I felt my way up by the wainscoting, because I didn't want to make a noise, and when I got to the top, I forgot what a deuced wide staircase it was, and when I turned to go towards my door, what does I do but walks right down stairs again, a good deal faster than I went up, and struck my head agin the corner-post, and be hanged to it! Bad eye, isn't it? And all from that infernal Elizabethan stairway."

We thought that the fault lay with the rum.

SEEKING A COMET.

It was with an anxious feeling that Mrs. Partington, having smoked her specs, directed her gaze towards the western sky, in quest of the tailless comet of 1850.

"I can't see it," said she; and a shade of vexation was perceptible in the tone of her voice. "I don't think much of this explanatory system," continued she, "that they praise so, where the stars are mixed up so that I can't tell Jew Peter from Satan, nor the consternation of the Great Bear from the man in the moon. 'Tis all dark to me. I don't believe there is any comet at all. Who ever heard of a comet without a tail, I should like to know? It isn't natural; but the printers will make a tale for it fast enough, for they are always getting up comical stories."

With a complaint about the falling dew, and a slight murmur of disappointment, the dame disappeared behind a deal door, like the moon behind a cloud.

Among the Roman priesthood was a class called *augurs*. There are many great *bores* among our modern priests.

BENEVOLENCE UNAPPRECIATED.

Philanthropos was at a public meeting one evening, where the heat was distressing, and, observing a lady on a seat in front of him who appeared to be suffering from excessive warmth, he went out and bought a large fan, which he delicately set in motion, as if fanning himself, while he made every effort to give her the benefit of the artificial breeze, becoming himself additionally heated from the exertion he made, losing all interest in the concert, from his intentness in the benevolent action, and smiling to himself with the belief that his kindness was felt, without its source being known. He was thus benevolently happy, until he heard the lady tell her husband to go and shut down that odious window behind her, for she had felt cold on her neck all the evening from the east wind. Philanthropos went out and sold the fan for seven coppers, that he had given a quarter for an hour before.

ON GHOSTS.

" Do you believe in ghosts, Mrs. Partington ?" it was asked of the old lady, somewhat timidly.

" To be sure I do," replied she, " as much as I believe that bright fulminary there will rise in the yeast to-morrow morning, if we live and nothing happens. Two apprehensions have sartainly appeared in our own family. Why, I saw my dear Paul, a fortnight before he died, with my own eyes, jest as plain as I see you now ; and though it turned out arterwards to be a rose-bush with a night-cap on it, I shall always think, to the day of my desolation, that it was a forerunner sent to me. 'T other one came in the night, when we were asleep, and carried away three candles and a pint of spirits that we kept in the house for an embarkation. Believe in ghosts, indeed! I guess I do, and he must be a dreadful styptic as doesn't ! " and she piously turned to the part of the Book relating to the witch of Endor.

STAGE COMPANIONSHIP.

SOME folks are always talking, and some, with provoking taciturnity, are always saying nothing, to use a left-handed expression. We like a good talker, intelligent, quick, ready,—whose happy conversational power tends to make the rough way of life pleasant ; and we have a corresponding dread of one who drones, and hesitates, and speaks only by monosyllables, and then as if he took out each word and looked at it before he dared to utter it. It is amusing at times to observe two of these human opposites come in contact,—to hear the lively laugh and playful jest of the one, as he rattles on, like a fast horse over the paving-stones, striking a spark at every step, and the sombre glumness of the other, who, hardly deigning to smile, sits tongueless, brooding over his thoughts, like a hen at midnight.   Put the two in a stage-coach or rail-car, to modernise a little, and see how the former will shine; while the latter, poor dummy, though perhaps morally and intellectually worth six of the former, sits unnoted, or regarded only as some cheap fellow of no consequence.

We were one of three who, one day long ago, occupied seats with the driver of a stage, during a fifty mile ride, and one of the company was the merriest fellow we ever saw.   He told stories, sung songs, and laughed, till all rang again, with our accompaniment, by the "dim woods" that we passed, and over the hills that we climbed.   It was a jolly ride, surpassing that, we think, of the renowned Mr. Pickwick, where the very correct Bob Sawyer occupied an equally outside position with our illustrious selves. We were somewhat inclined to be merry in those days, may Heaven forgive us! and that ride was an event to be remembered life-long.   The whole party enjoyed it, save one, and he was the most woebegone-looking customer we had ever seen.   Joking wouldn't move him; he was impenetrable to any missile of that kind, and there he sat with a countenance of fifty miles long,—'t is fair to reckon it by the length of the road,—gazing very sadly at the right ear of the nigh horse.   Our funny companion at last bent his whole battery upon the silent man, and tried to draw him out.   It was an entire failure, and the joker, a little chagrined at the other's imperturbability, asked him, in a somewhat hasty tone, why the (something) he didn't talk.   Without moving his eyes from the contemplation of the horse's ear, he opened his head, and these words dropped out: " *What's—the—use—of—talking?* "

MR. SLOW UPON MORAL WORTH.

" 'BIMELECH, you must try and be a good man—I've always taught you that.   Never let your name be at a discount on 'change; always mind and take up your notes, 'cause credit's everything in the world.   What's a man without credit?   He a'n't nothing—he a'n't nowhere.   For a man to be without credit is about as bad as poverty, and a man without money or credit is to be despised.   Avoid such people as you would the small-pox. Look at your gran'ther.   'Bimelech; there's a sample for you to follow.   He always acted right.   He never owed a shilling, an' never lost one, 'cause he was shrewd. He never run round, lending his money to folks—not he. Morgidges did it; and people used to love to have him foreclose on 'em, 'cause he did it so good-naturedly. He was a *good* man. His name was always right on 'change. *He* could always get money, let it be ever so hard. You never catched him squandering his money on charitable humbugs, and encouraging porpoises—not he; and when he died he was worth two thousand a-year, and the ships' colours were histed half-mast, 'cause a good man had fell in Israel! " 'Bimelech must improve under such training, and isn't it the world's teaching continually ?

MR. SLOW OFF SOUNDINGS.

" THE airth is round, my son," said Mr. Slow, impressively, taking an apple from Abimelech's hand, and holding it up between his thumb and finger, " like a napple, and revolves on its own axle-tree round the sun, jest as reg'lar as any machine you ever see. The airth is made up of land, and water, and rocks, besides vegetation and trees, and things growing. The mountings upon the service of the earth are very high,—more 'n a half a mile, I should think; some of 'em are called white mountings, because they a'n't black. The ocean is very deep, and some folks thinks it hasn't got no bottom. This is all gammon. Everything has got a bottom, my son. The reason they can't find it is 'cause the world is round. They throw their sinker overboard, and it goes right through one side, like this "—(thrusting his knife through the apple),—" and hangs down underneath, jest so, Of course they can't find a bottom.

Mr. Slow gave his boy the apple, and turned round, much satisfied with himself.

AN EDITOR A LITTLE HEATED,

COPY! quotha? copy!—with the thermometer at 90°! What an unconscionable dog it is, to be sure, to worry one so. Not one line, so help us Stebbings!—not one line. Avaunt! quit our sight! for the heat of the day is fused into our spirit, and,

" By that sword which gleams above us,"

annihilation awaits you, if you dare provoke us with your impostunity. The idea of writing at such time is abominable, and no reasonable devil would insist on't. A vile knave thou art at best, with thy swart and lank jaws there distended, bawling for copy. Grin away, you waif from the lake of Tartarus, whose burning flood ne'er yielded a more hideous whelp for our, or the world's, torment. We tell thee, swart minion, vile Mercury of inordinate jours, that copy thou canst not have. What! write when the atmosphere, like hot lava, wreathes the brow and sticks there with the tenacity of molten pitch, and burns and burns upon the brain like the thirst for revenge, or the seething scald of impending pecuniary obligation? Away, caitiff! and "tell thy masters this, and tell them, too," that we will see them hanged ere we will write a line for them to-day. Vamose! mizzle! scatter! or, by St. Paul, temper, outraged, shall take to itself form, and launch its thunders on thy devoted head! But, stay. This, the ebullition of our wrath, is copy, poor at best,—give it 'em.

DON'T CUT IT, MISS.

"DON'T you think my dress much too long?" asked Seraphina, the youngest of the seven, of old Roger.

"Don't cut it, miss, even if it is. I beg of you, as a friend, not to cut it," said the old man seriously.

"Why not?" inquired she, timidly.

"Because, miss, I remember a difficulty of my own once, under like circumstances, which was a source of much shame to me. Overtaken by a severe shower far from home, I was terribly drenched, and a new pair of sheepskin inexpressibles that I wore, tied close at the knee, as was the fashion then, received the dripping streams from my body, and, distended like a bad case of the dropsy, fell below my calves; like your dress, they were too long, and I cut them off at the knee. But the warm sun came out, the sheepskin contracted; inch by inch I felt it creeping up my legs; and, by the time I got home, you may be sure I was a sight to behold. Don't cut it, miss, unless you feel perfectly sure it will not shrink more."

There was a smile at the old gentleman's delicacy in the matter, but there could be no fear of danger, and they didn't see how the cases were parallel at all.

TWENTY-NINE CATS.

" Scat!" screamed Mrs. Partington, from the head of the stairs, as the noise of an interesting quadruped of the cat species in the kitchen below met her ears. " Scat! I say!"

She listened to ascertain the result of her command; but the noise was resumed, and the little kitchen echoed again with the feline music,—spitting, and mewing, and growling with the concatenation of malignity in every note of it that reached her as she leaned over the bannister.

" Gracious Heaven!" cried she, " I should think there was twenty of 'em; what *shall* I do? Scat!" she screamed again, and the noise redoubled; indeed, it appeared to her excited fancy that a reinforcement had arrived, and were all in full chorus, and now the crash of crockery added to her fear. She dared not go down, for, of all things in the world, she feared a spiteful cat. It became suddenly still in a moment or so, and she ventured down stairs. A broken plate was on the floor, with traces of molasses upon the fragments, and Ike very demurely sat behind the stove, counting his marbles.

" Has there been any cats in here, Isaac?" said the kind old lady, looking anxiously round the room.

" Twenty-seven, twenty-eight, twenty-nine"—

" Where, for goodness' sake, did twenty-nine cats come from?" asked she; " but I knowed there was a good many of 'em."

" And there's a twoser," continued Ike, still counting, " and a Chinese."

" Anything like the Maltees, Isaac?" inquired she.

" I mean marbles, aunt," said Ike.

" And I mean cats, Isaac," said Mrs. Partington, severely.

It was a scene for a painter,—Coffin should do it up,—her eyes alternated between the broken plate and the boy, as if pondering the mystery of the sounds she had heard, and Ike wiped the molasses from his mouth on his sleeve. Didn't the molasses on the plate explain it? He had to take a lecture, you may depend, on the certainty of roguish boys being awfully punished for plaguing the aged, and he had to read the story aloud, before he went to bed that night, of the boys who were eaten up by the she-bears.

A coach containing a young man and woman with one trunk on behind,—behind the coach is meant,—is pleasingly suggestive of matrimony.

"Yes," says old Roger, sardonically, "but a half-dozen young ones and seven bandboxes are much more suggestive,—there's no mistaking signs like those."

MRS. PARTINGTON ON TOBACCO.

"I know that tobacco is very dilatorious," said Mrs. Partington, as Mr. Trask sat conversing with her upon the body and soul destroying nature of the weed. "I know that tobacco is dilatorious, especially to a white floor;" and, taking out her snuff-box,—the broad one with the picture of Napoleon on the cover,—she tapped it, and offered a pinch to her guest.

"Snuff is just as bad," said he, laying his finger gently on her arm and speaking earnestly—"snuff injures the intellect, affects the nerves, destroys the memory; it is *tobacco* in its most subtle form, and the poison appears as the devil did in Eden, under a pleasing exterior."

She gazed upon him a moment in silence.

"I know," said she, "it has a tenderness to the head; but I couldn't do without it, it is so auxiliarating to me when I am down to the heel; and if it is a pizen, as you call it, I should have been killed by it forty years ago. Good snuff, like good tea, is a great blessing, and I don't see how folks who have no amusement can get along without it."

The box was dropped back to its receptacle, and her friend took his leave, sighing that she would persist in shortening her days by the use of snuff, and stopped a moment to lecture Ike, who was enjoying a sugar cigar upon the front door-step.

GUITAR IN THE HEAD.

MRS. PARTINGTON'S neighbour, Mrs. Sled, complained one morning of a ringing in her ears.

"It must be owing to the guitar in your head, dear," said the old lady. She knew every sort of human ailment, and, like the down-cast doctor, was death on fits. "I know what ringing in the ears is," continued she; "for my ears used to ring so bad, sometimes, as to wake Paul out of his sleep, thinking it was an alarm of fire!"

There was no doubt she was telling what was true, but there were some that questioned it in a gentle cough. We haven't a doubt of its truth.

A SINGULAR FACT.

"THEM are very fat critters," remarked Mrs. Partington, as she stood viewing a yoke of splendid steers.

"Yes 'm," replied the farmer, "and, would you believe it, mum, they were fattened on nothin' but oat straw, and it hadn't been threshed, neither."

"You don't say so!" said she, and, for a moment, doubt of the probability of the story occupied her mind; it was but for a moment. "Well, I never!" continued she, and turned aside to admire the beauties of a new cider-press.

A HIT AT THE TIMES.

"BRED by steam-power!" screamed Mrs. Partington, as she heard Isaac commence a paragraph about making bread by steam. She laid down her work, placed her hands upon her lap, and looked broadly at the boy through her specs. "Bred by steam!" said she; "what will the world do next? I wonder if this is one of the labour-saving inventions, now. But I see what it will end in. People are fast enough now, in all conscience; but what will they do when they come to be bred by steam-power, if they act according to their bringing up? Ah, Isaac, people may be faster now, but they are no better than they used to be!"

Isaac explained that it was a new mode of making bread. She looked at him steadily for a moment, when, taking a thumb and finger full, she put the cover on the box, resumed her knitting, and told Isaac to go on, which he did.

MR. SLOW ON GRAVE TOPICS.

"'BIMELECH, my son," said Mr. Slow, shaking his head with oracular and owl-like profundity, "it isn't well to know too much, my boy; your father never did—he know'd too much for that. Thoughts is perplexin', and the human mind, 'Bimelech, is too precious a thing to be wore out with too much friction. Don't abuse the gifts of nater, my son, 'cause nater's one of 'em, she is. Don't investigate anything new, my boy, 'cause there's a thousand old things of more consekence to look arter—the first of which is number one. New notions perplexes the mind, dear —there's full enough fools in the world who like to look arter sich things, without your troublin' your precious head about 'em—

't wouldn't be a cent of benefit to you. Call 'em all humbug and moonshine, and them as believes 'em lunatics and scoundrels, and that 'll save you a good many discussions, and give you a character for dignity and prudence; and prudent folks make money. Phelosophy and scions, and them things, is humbugs, and everything is humbug but money. Mind, I tell ye." Mr. Slow ceased, overcome by his own eloquence.

PAYING AN OLD DEBT.

Working out a debt is often called " working a dead horse," and we think not inaptly, the more especially when a man is poor, with a family depending upon him for support; then a pickaxe becomes a weary thing, and every shovel-full of dirt weighs four times as much as when the heart of the labourer is cheered by the hope of the shilling a-head. But it is well to pay one's debts; though it is far better not to owe anything—a piece of advice that St. Paul utters with great earnestness, as if he were practically sensible of the disadvantage of indebtedness.

A man who had run up a long score at a shop for liquor, cigars, and other creature comforts, found himself utterly unable to pay a stiver of it. In vain was he urged to pay the bill, and in vain was he threatened if he didn't; he hadn't any money,—the true secret of his getting in debt in the first place,—and the creditor gave it up. At last he thought he would compromise the matter, and let the man work the debt out. The creditor had a large pile of wood in his barn, several cords of it, nicely sawed and split, and he forthwith set the debtor at work to throw the wood into the street and then pile it back again, at the rate of a shilling an hour, until the whole debt should be wiped out. The man took hold with a will, and, in a short time, the wood was all in the street; then it went back with equal celerity and then out again, and then in; everybody wondering what it could mean. Some charitably intimated that he was crazy, and others, equally charitable, said he was drunk. He toiled on thus the whole day, throwing the wood back and forth, but every hour seemed full sixty minutes longer than its predecessor, as he watched the clock on the old church in the neighbourhood. He was working a dead horse, and it was hard making him go. But the longest road must have an end, and the hour neared when the labour and debt would cease together, and, as the hammer of the clock told the hour of his release, the freed man threw the last stick of wood into the street with a shout of triumph. The shout brough the owner of the wood to the door, who found his late debtor putting on his coat to go away.

"Halloo!" said he, "you are not going away without putting the wood back again, are you?"

"I'll put it back again for a shilling an hour," said the man.

The proprietor of the wood saw that he had been done, but good-naturedly told his late creditor to go ahead and put it back. He went about it; but, strange to say, it took him just three times as long to put it back as it did to throw it out.

MRS. PARTINGTON having been asked what the consequences would be if an irresistible should come in contact with an immoveable body, replied that she thought one or t'other of 'em would get hurt.

OPERATIC REBUKE.

"I CAN'T catch the malady!" said Mrs. Partington, at the opera, as she stood upon tiptoe, in the lobby of the Howard Athenæum, in vain attempting to look over the heads before her. She had received a ticket, but it secured nothing but an outside position, and she had gone wandering round like a jolly planet without any particular orbit. Ike was in the gallery, eating a penny's worth of pea-nuts, and throwing the shells into the parquet below. "I can't catch the malady of the uproar, and more 'n half the words are all Dutch to me. This is the first opiatic performance I ever went to, and if I can't get a seat, I can't stand it to come agin."

She said it very firmly. As she was going down the stairs, a young gentleman, with curly hair, reached over the bannisters, and blandly informed her that he could furnish her with a seat. She turned her benevolent spectacles, and face attached, towards him, and told him it was rather late, after the evening had half gone, to think of politeness.

It was a picture! The young curly head bending over the bannister, and the spectacles, and the black bonnet, and the widow of Corporal Paul, on the stairs looking up. It was sublime!

A WOMAN THAT ONE COULD LOVE.

"Now, there is a woman that one could love," said old Roger, delightedly, as he saw a figure, arrayed in the full feather of fashion, in a window in Regent Street. "A long life could be spent very quietly in such company; no quarrelling for precedence; no jealousy; no strife of any kind ; no teasing for dress and follies, till one's purse-strings ache in sympathy with aching heart-strings, at unchecked extravagance. Even I could love such a woman as that."

"Perhaps you could," responded a sweet voice at his side; "but would it love you back again, think you? There would be no return for your investment of affection here in this heartless thing, this mere frame; you should turn your attention to something worthy of your love, where, for a small outlay of affection, a tenfold return would be made you in domestic joy."

"Alas!" said the old bachelor, "where shall I find this?"

But the beautiful eyes that met his proved how easily the question might be answered; and, with a melancholy step, he passed along. He was more a bachelor from habit than from choice, after all.

INTRODUCING THE WATER.

"Bless me!" exclaimed Mrs. Partington, coming in out of breath, and dropping down into a chair, like a jolly old kedge anchor, at the same time fanning herself with an imaginary fan. She did not say "Bless me," because she was in want of any particular blessing at that time; it was merely an ejaculation of hers, expressive of deep emotion. "Bless me!" said she, "I don't see why the Water Commissionaries were so much worried and fretted about introducing the Cochituate water for; I think it is the easiest thing in the world to get acquainted with. Look at that bonnet, now," holding up the antiquated, but well-preserved bit o' crape, dripping with watery drops, like the umbrella of Aquarius; "look at that bonnet, now! ruined to all tents and porpoises by the pesky water-works. Introduce it, indeed!" continued she, ironically, looking severely at the wrecked article in her hand, "'t'an't no use of introducing an acquaintance that makes so free with you at first sight."

She arose to hang up her bonnet, when Ike, who was hanging upon the back of her chair, fell heavily against the window, and thrust the rear portion of his person through four panes of glass.

"O, Isaac!" said she, "you'll be the ruination of me. If I was rich as Creosote I couldn't stand it."

Isaac gathered himself from among the fragments of glass, and seemed quite tickled with an idea that he could sell the pieces, in conjunction with a reserve of old iron, and half of the clothes-line, and three junk bottles, to raise funds for the Fourth of July.

RATHER FUNNY.

OLD ROGER was standing in State Street, and saw an Irishman rolling a keg of specie from his cart to the institution for which it was intended.

"There," said the old fellow to a foreign gentleman who was standing by him, "there you see the benefit of our free institutions; there is a man who came to this country six months ago, as poor as poor could be, and now, you see, he is actually rolling in riches!"

He said this, and turned round, very red in the face, and struck his cane several times violently on the sidewalk, and waited for his friend to explode. Hearing no sign of cachination, he turned and found the gentleman vainly endeavouring to decipher the emblems on the Merchants' Exchange. He evidently hadn't understood the joke.

ON ONE STRING.

"THE Music of Paganini executed on one string!" said Mrs. Partington. "Praying, I s'pose, to be cut down. Poor Paganini!" sighed she; "executed on one string! Well, I don't know as ever I heard of anybody's being executed on two strings, unless the rope broke;" and she went on wondering how it could be.

SEEKING THE LIGHT.

"I DECLARE, I don't know what to think on it!" said Mrs. Partington as she looked intently into the water-pail. The attitude was peculiar, and the iron-bowed specs were on duty, like a sentry on a bridge, keeping a bright look-out over the water.

"I can't see into it."

This was wrong if we take it literally, because the water was as pure and transparent as her own benevolence.

"I can't see into it, and the more I preponderate upon it, the more I'm in a bewilderness. How Mr. Paine can make light of water is more than I can see,—I can't throw no light on it. I know it's made of some sort of gin. My poor Paul's head used to be made light by gin and water, but it didn't burn, as they say this will."

Her listeners stood hatless, almost breathless, as her voice came up through her cap-border, like the steam from around the cover of a wash-boiler, while Ike put the experiment to a practical test, by pouring a dipper of water into the stove.

JUDGING VIRTUE BY ITS SMELL.

"It smells virtuous," said Mrs. Partington, as she smelt of the hartshorn bottle that had long lain away in an old-fashioned high closet, before which the old lady stood, on a tall chair, exploring the dark interior of the receptacle for "unconsidered trifles." "It smells virtuous." We had often heard of the peculiar *odour* of goodness, that rises like frankincense amid an atmosphere of vice; and here was a practical application that attested the justness of the term. It was sublime! and the figure standing there on the high chair, like Truth on a pedestal, with the specs, and the close cap, and the blue yarn stockings, formed a subject for a sculptor, poorer than which had immortalised hundreds.

ABUSES OF THE PRESS.

"The printing-press is a great steam-engine," said Mrs. Partington; "but I don't believe Dr. Franklin ever invented it to commit outrages on a poor female woman like me. It makes me say everything, Mrs. Sled; and some of the things I know must have been said when I was *out*, for I can't remember 'em;" and she dropped three stitches in her excitement. "They ought to think," continued she, "that them who makes sport of the aged don't never live to grow up."

MOUSE-HUNTING;

AN INCIDENT IN THE LIFE OF MRS. PARTINGTON.

It was midnight, deep and still, in the mansion of Mrs. Partington,—as it was, very generally, about town,—on a cold night in March. So profound was the silence, that it awakened Mrs. P., and she raised herself upon her elbow to listen. No sound

greeted her ears, save the tick of the old wooden clock in the
next room, which stood there in the dark, like an old chrone,
whispering and gibbering to itself. Mrs. Partington relapsed
beneath the folds of the blankets, and had one eye again well-
coaxed towards the realm of dreams, while the other was holding
by a very frail tenure upon the world of reality, when her ear
was saluted by the nibble of a mouse, directly beneath her chamber window, and the mouse was evidently gnawing her chamber
carpet.

Now, if there is an animal in the catalogue of creation that she
dreads and detests, it is a mouse ; and she has a vague and inde-
finite idea that rats and mice were made with especial regard to
her individual torment. As she heard the sound of the nibble by
the window, she rose again upon her elbow, and cried "*Shoo !
Shoo !*" energetically, several times. The sound ceased, and she
fondly fancied that her trouble was over. Again she laid herself
away as carefully as she would have lain eggs at two shillings a
dozen, when,—*nibble, nibble, nibble !*—she once more heard the
odious sound by the window. "*Shoo !*" cried the old lady again,
at the same time hurling her shoe at the spot from whence the
sound proceeded, where the little midnight marauder was carrying on his depredations.

A light burned upon the hearth,—she couldn't sleep without a
light,—and she strained her eyes in vain to catch a glimpse of
her tormentor playing about amid the shadows of the room. All
again was silent, and the clock, giving an admonitory tremble,
struck twelve. Midnight! and Mrs. Partington counted the tin-
tinabulous knots as they ran off the reel of Time, with a saddened
heart.

Nibble, nibble, nibble !—again that sound. The old lady sighed,
as she hurled the other shoe at her invisible annoyance. It was
all without avail, and "shooing" was bootless, for the sound
came again to her wakeful ear. At this point her patience gave
out, and, conquering her dread of the cold, she arose and opened
the door of her room that led to a corridor, when, taking the
light in one hand, and a shoe in the other, she made the circuit
of the room, and explored every nook and cranny in which a
mouse could ensconce himself. She looked under the bed, and
under the old chest of drawers, and under the washstand, and
"shooed" until she could "shoo" no more.

The reader's own imagination, if he has an imagination skilled
in limning, must draw the picture of the old lady while upon
this exploring expedition, "accoutred as she was," in search of
the ridiculous mouse. We have our own opinion upon the sub-

ject, and must say,—with all due deference to the years and virtues of Mrs. P., and with all regard for personal attractions, very striking in one of her years,—we should judge that she cut a very queer figure, indeed.

Satisfying herself that the mouse must have left the room, she closed the door, deposited the light upon the hearth, and again sought repose. How grateful a warm bed feels, when exposure to the night air has chilled us, as we crawl to its enfolding covert! How we nestle down, like an infant by its mother's breast, and own no joy superior to that we feel,—coveting no regal luxury while revelling in the elysium of feathers! So felt Mrs. P., as she again ensconced herself in bed. The clock in the next room struck one.

She was again near the attainment of the state when dreams are rife, when, close by her chamber-door, outside, she heard that hateful nibble renewed which had marred her peace before. With a groan she arose, and, seizing her lamp, she opened the door, and had the satisfaction to hear the mouse drop, step by step, until he reached the floor below. Convinced that she was now rid of him for the night, she returned to bed, and addressed herself to sleep. The room grew dim; in the weariness of her spirit, the chest of drawers in the corner was fast losing its identity and becoming something else ; in a moment more——*nibble, nibble, nibble!* again outside of the chamber-door, as the clock in the next room struck two.

Anger, disappointment, desperation, fired her mind with a new determination. Once more she arose, but this time she put on a shoe!—her dexter shoe. Ominous movement! It is said that when a woman wets her finger, fleas had better flee. The star of that mouse's destiny was setting, and was now near the horizon. She opened the door quickly, and, as she listened a moment, she heard him drop again from stair to stair, on a speedy passage down.

The entry below was closely secured, and no door was open to admit of his escape. This she knew, and a triumphant gleam shot athwart her features, revealed by the rays of the lamp. She went slowly down the stairs, until she arrived at the floor below, where, snugly in a corner, with his little bead-like black eyes looking up at her roguishly, was the gnawer of her carpet, and the annoyer of her comfort. She moved towards him, and he, not coveting the closer acquaintance, darted by her. She pursued him to the other end of the entry, and again he passed by her. Again and again she pursued him, with no better success. At last, when in most doubt as to which side would conquer, Fortune, perched upon the bannister, turned the scale in favour of Mrs. P. The mouse, in an attempt to run by her, presumed too much upon former success. He came too near her upraised foot. It fell upon his musipilar beauties, like an avalanche of snow upon a new tile, and he was dead for ever! Mrs. Partington gazed upon him as he lay before her. Though she was glad at the result, she could but sigh at the necessity which impelled the violence; but for which the mouse might have long continued a blessing to the society in which he moved.

> Slowly and sadly she marched up stairs,
>   With her shoe all sullied and gory;
> And the watch, who saw't through the front door squares,
>   Told us this part of the story.

That mouse did not trouble Mrs. Partington again that night, and the old clock in the next room struck three before sleep again visited the eyelids of the relict of Corporal Paul.

STAR-GAZING.

Out beneath the starry heavens Mr. Slow took his son, Abimelech, to point out to him—to read to him from the broad page of nature—the wonders of

"The spacious *furnishment* on high,"

as he called it.

"All these 'ere stars, my son," said Mr. S., pointing up to the studded sky above them, "that you see up there, stationary and unmoveable, marchin' along in sublime grande'r, and winking at the earth with their jolly yeller eyes, like gold eagles, them are called *fixed* stars;' and"—

"But what's that, father?" said young Abimelech, as a meteor, like a racer, darted across the southerly sky.

Mr. Slow was prompt with his answer.

"That," said he, "I guess, is one of 'em that's got unfixed."

MRS. P. ON MOUNT VESUVIUS.

"So there's been another rupture of Mount Vociferous!" said Mrs. Partington, as she put down the paper and put up her specs. "The paper tells all about the burning lather running down the mountain, but it don't tell us how it got afire. I won-

der if it was set fire to. There are many people full wicked
enough to do it, or, perhaps, it was caused by children playing
with frictious matches. I wish they had sent for our firemen;
they would soon have put a stop to the raging aliment; and I
dare say Mr. Barnacle, and all of 'em, would have gone, for they
are what I call real civil engineers."

There was a whole broadside of commendation of the fire de-
partment in the impressive gesture accompanying her words.
" Time and space " for a moment became annihilated, and imagination figured the city engines pouring their subduing streams
upon the flames of Vesuvius; and " Hold on, seving! " " Break
her down, twelve! " rising above the vain roarings of the smother-
ing crater.

THE PIC-NIC:

A GRAND DOMESTIC DRAMA,

IN MANY ACTS.

*In which are detailed the Fun and Drawbacks attending a Pleasure Excursion
in the town of Bozzleton.*

PERSONS IN THE DRAMA.

Mr. Homespun—Who has something to say to all, and about everybody.
Jemima Short—A sweet little country rose.
Mr. Blisby—A gentleman from the city.
Miss Primrose—A refined lady of thirty-five, full of sentiment and some snuff.
Mr. Brindle—A bachelor of fifty-eight, and a justice of the peace.
Miss Pidgin—A bird too tough for sentiment.
  Auxiliaries, Horses, Pigeon Pie, &c., by the company.

  The morn is bright in Bozzleton, and kindly beams the sun,
  And spreads his choicest rays around as if he dreamt of fun;
  The girls are up and wide awake, the lads are spruce and gay,
  For a pic-nic party is arranged for this bright summer day.

AND won't we have a time of it? Just see the bag of doughnuts that Jemima Short has thrown out of the window into the
wagon! And there go three chickens, and four pies, and a jug
of cider. Goodness gracious, Jemima! You are an angel of a
provider, you are! You don't mean to put us on a regiment to-
day, do you? You look like an airthly goddess, too, in your new
pink calico. I vow, it looks first-rate—I took it for chinchilli a
rod off.

Jemima.—" I don't know—I don't think much of it, but folks
tells me it's becoming. Miss Jeems, the milliner, got the pattern
from the city, and ——"

How de do, Miss Short? Gwine to the pic-nic?

Mrs. S. (with a cold in her head.)—"No, guess not; don't feel smart, 'zactly, and the old man 's got the romantic affection in his leg, and can't go nuther; but Mima is gwine; she has had her hair in papers a whole week to make her look pretty."

Jemima.—"Why, mother! how you do talk! But here they come—O, what a host of 'em! How proud Betsey Babb feels of her new dress! I guess some folks can look full as well as some folks; and there's that everlasting old maid, Miss Pidgin: how I hate her with her scraggy neck and long tongue! And there' Patty Sprigg's city beau—O, I wouldn't be *her* to be seen with such a fright!"

> The wagons packed with eatables go groaning o'er the road,
> The long carts filled with girls and beaus show an attractive load,
> And laughter rules the pleasant hour, and eyes shine gay and bright,
> The only kind of stars that show as well by day as night.

Laughter! guess you'd think so to hear it. Now the cart settles down into a rut. "Dear me," says Miss Tibbs, "we shall all be upsot, tipsy-turvy; do hold on to me!" and then everybody thinks they must be held on to; and everybody else is trying to hold on to somebody. O, how frightened the city beauty is! "Do you apprehend any danger of a tergiversation?" "No," says Jo Hays, "the slack men look arter them things, and everybody's noclated for it."

Female Voice.—"Be still, won't you! O, you satan! see how you have tumbled my collar with your pesky nonsense; and my face burns like fire-coals. Right before a city gentleman, too; O, for shame!"

City Gent.—"Upon my honour, miss, I was entirely oblivious to any impropriety."

"O, 't wasn't very improper either, he, he, he; only such things shouldn't be done publicly, you know."

Miss Pidgin.—"If Susan Fry isn't setting on Sam Sled's knees, I a'n't a living sinner! Such conduct I must think improper. *I* never was guilty of such indiscretion, *I* never was!"

Boys singing—

> "There's fun in a country cart,
>   And life on a dusty road,
> Where mirth warms every heart,
>   And pleasure finds abode:
> The town may boast of its joys,
>   Its racket and its din,
> But give a haunt away from its noise,
>   Some quiet nook within."

Far from the busy din of town, in some secluded grove,
The happy party sit them down, or unrestricted rove ;
All austere rules that bind the world are here thrown far aside,
And revelling in mirth's bright beam, how fleet the moments glide !

Arm-in-arm under the shady trees they now wander, picking posies or bright berries—and *such* fun ! Miss Primrose smiles languidly a sort of sky-blue benignity upon old Brindle, the bachelor.

Miss Primrose (sentimentally). — " How delightfully those pines sigh in the gentle breeze, like the soft music of love in the ear of youth ! "

Old Brindle.—" Yes'm, so it does."

Miss P.—" O, I do so love the pines ! "

Old B.—" They're better in May, mum, when the sliver is thick and creamy. Come out here then, marm, out with your jack-knife, throw away your tobacco, cut out a square, and sliver *up* the tree—allers sliver up, marm—some slivers down. Then's when you'd like the pines, mum."

Miss P.—" That's an entirely new aspect; I meant their romantic beauty."

Old B.—" Yes'm—beautiful wood, very ; worth four dollars a cord in Boston."

Here come Patty Sprig and the musty-choked man from the city.

Cit.—" Miss Spwig, how delightfully ruwal it is here ! Always thought I should like to live among the beauties of Nachure. It's a great pity we can't have any nachure in town, a great pity. I've heard of some *human* nachure round there, but never saw any of it."

Patty.—" I should think they might bring it in by pipes, as they did the Cochituate."

Cit.—" Are those gwound nuts ? "

Patty.—" No, dear me, no; don't eat 'em; they're toddstools."

Thus we go on, chatting, walking,
Voices ringing with the pines,
Nothing our gay fancies balking,
Doing all our heart inclines.

Now on the green and beauteous sod the varied viands spread,
And appetite shall wait on health, and wit its influence shed ;
The social tongue with music rife blends with the platter's noise,
As earth's rude jarring interferes with its harmonious joys.

" Here's tongue, and ham, and sausages, and pumkin pie, and cheese. Mercy, what a bill of fare ! Miss Peewit, shall I help

you to a piece of tongue?"—"No, thank you, I have enough of my own. But I'll trouble you for a piece of the chicken."
—"Chicken, did you say? From his toughness I should say he was a grandfather to thousands!"

"Pass the pigeon yonder, will you?"

'What, the old maid?"

"No, no, the pie."

"There's the plate—the pigeon is unavoidably detained."

Miss Pidgin.—"I'd thank people who use my name to speak so that I can hear; I don't like to be backbitten."

"We were speaking of pigeon pie, mem — *something more tender* (aside).

"Say, Tom, what have you got in the dish there?"

"Pickled grasshoppers, I should think. Will you have some?"

"Miss Primrose, do allow me to help you; here's some ham, delicate as your own nature, ma'am."

Miss P.—"I declare, you are quite complimentary! Comparing my nature with smoked hog!"

"Will Mr. Blisby, the gentleman from the city, favour us with a song? Silence, 'ye gentlemen and ladies all that grace this famous pic-nic; Mr. Blisby is going to sing."

Mr. B.—"I'd rather be excused; but though I am not exactly in tune, I'll endeavour for the occasion."

Mr. Blisby sings :—

> "My love is fair, O, she is fair!
>   Her lips are red, her eyes like sloe,
> A golden glory is her hair,
>   Falling o'er shoulders white as snow.
> And when her eyes upon me turn,
>   And burn with radiance divine,
> My ardent gaze encounters hern,
>   The same as hern encounters mine."

Child, yelling.—"Mother, give me a nuther pieth ov pie!
Mother.—"Hush, my darling, there a'n't any."
Boy—"I thay there ith; I want a pieth ov pie!"

> "O, such a mingling
>   Of talking and jingling,
>   The noise and glee
>   Sound merrily,
> And set our ears a tingling."

A dance! a dance! and gleefully a set is forthwith planned,
A fiddle most mysteriously has happened here at hand;
And here beneath the dark tree's shade, with leaves and berries crown'd,
Each happy lad and laughing maid whirl in the dance around.

"Go it, my top sawyer on the pussy gut! Work your elbows lively, and we'll put her through by daylight!" "O, dear! I'm all of a perspiration with sweat. How slippery it is under foot!" "It a'n't slippery anywheres else." "I swow to man, there's Bill Nutter and Jemima Short both down! Up and try it again, clumsies!"

Miss Primrose.—"How these old woods echo with the music, Mr. Brindle, like the Arcadian groves, with the dulcet notes of the Satires!"

Mr. B.—"I never heerd of 'em; I guess they never was in these woods—they never was that I can remember."

"I declare, there's Mr. Blisby dancing like an animated bean-pole. Ha! ha! ha! he's on all-fours. Now all he wants is a tail."

Then moving to the tuning of the fiddle and the bow,
How sparkles every eye with mirth as round and round we go!
No ball-room artistes now are here to circumscribe our sport,
And Nature smiles approvingly, for here she holds her court.

A lake romantic lying near tempts to its cooling vale,
And tiny boats in swift career across its bosom sail;
And waving handkerchiefs respond in answer to the song
That, rising from the venturers, is borne the breeze along.

"Jump into the boat, Patty; not the least danger in the world of its tipping over."—"O, my! I've got my shoe all satiated with water. I shall get my death a cold."—"You've got your foot in it this time, that's a fact."

Mr. Blisby—"Is there any danger of sea-sickness?"

"Now just see that boat—how she scoots it! I vow if Patty Sprig hasn't got hold of the bow oar, and pulls away like a little satan. If I thought that spindle-shank from the city was going to have that gal, I'd cut his eternal—acquaintance, I would. I e'enamost said throat, but that would be manslaughter; and I don't see how it could be, neither, for killing such a thing as he is."

A Voice.—"Some love to roam
O'er the dark sea's foam,
Where the shrill winds whistle free."

"Well, they do. Hallo! here's Jim Sly. What have you got in that bottle, old fellow? Haven't seen you to-day afore."

Jim Sly (drunk).—"I've got some c-c-cough drops to c-c-cure the sea-sickness with—a little rum t-t-t-tea with s-s-some sperrit in it to k-k-keep it."

Sally Twist, his sweetheart.—" You Jim Sly, you drunken, miserable fellow, you—you sot—you brute—you individual—you —you—you Jim Sly"——

Jim.—" Go it, S-S-Sal, and I'll hold your b-b-bonnet! What yer goin' to d-d-do 'bout it?"

Sally.—" You'll see when we get home, you sot—you brute— you vagabone!"

Sam.—" Let her lean, elder—'

> ' Wine cures the gout, boys,
> The colic, and the'——

sea-sickness. Who cares for S-S-Sall?"

" Can you tell me, Jemima, why Miss Pidgin yonder. is like forty-nine big apples?"—"No, I'm sure I can't, unless it's 'cause she's sour."—" No, 'ta'n't it; it's 'cause she's a vergin' nigh fifty."

> But gracious! what an awful cloud has risen in the west !
> And what a frightful lightning flash then swept across its breast !
> I feel a drop upon my hand—the pine trees rock and roar—
> The waves like blacks, with nightcaps on, rush madly to the shore!

" O, what *shall* we do? where *shall* we go? what *will* become of us?" screams everybody. "Do, dear Mr. Wiggin," says Miss Pidgin, "tell us *what* we shall do?"

Mr. Wiggin.—" Why, 'ta'n't no use to run's I see, for the rain is here, and there a'n't a house within a mile: and my 'pinion is that we get in the woods and make ourselves comfortable."

" But don't the lightnin' always strike trees?"

" There's more danger from your eyes, Jemima. Lightnin's attracted by anything bright; you'd better shut 'em up."

Jemima.—" Your wit isn't bright enough to attract it, any how, Mr. Impudence! How does that strike ye?"

Old Mrs. Fog.—" O, that folks should joke and trifle so, when there's so much to make 'em solemn! A'n't you afraid the thunder 'll kill you? And where would you go if you died a laughing?"

> The rain pours down in torrent force among the forest shades,
> And timid men the closer cling to timid, shrinking maids ;
> The whitened cheek and blenching eye denote the force of fear,
> And many a head bows low with dread the thunder loud to hear.

" Well, this is a comfort! See where Miss Primrose has cornered old Brindle—cheek-by-jowl. That's right. Go it, old gall!

My eyes! how it rains! If Pan is the presiding genius of these woods, in my opinion he's a dripping Pan."

Old Brindle.—"Young man, I'm a justice of the peace in this 'ere jurisdiction, and if you commit that agin, I shall commit you for contempt of court."

"Here comes Jim Sly through the wet, pitching like a mackerel-catcher in a chop sea. Hallo, Jim, here's Sally, like a widowed hen, refusing to be comforted."

Jim (sobered).—"Sally, will ye forgive me?"

Sally.—"No, you disreputable individual. To think that you should go away, and—and—leave me to—boo—hoo—hoo"——

Jim.—"There, don't cry, and I'll go and take the totetal pledge, Maine liquor law and all, and become a useful membrane of society, and if I drink any more, I hope I may never— starve!"

"See, Mr. Blisby, while we are soaking, how the horses outside are smoking."

Mr. B.—"Do horses in the country smoke?"

"Yes, and we've got a filly at home who throws all that choose to back her."

"You don't say so!"

> Thus, while the rain is pouring so,
> Fun may mingle with our fear:
> And, while the wind is roaring so,
> Still may waken words of cheer.

The rain clears up, the burnished sun comes out with scorching ray,
Dispelling from the sky and heart all shapes of gloom away,
And laughter now bursts forth once more in cheerful merry peal,
And "Home Again" is sung with glee as o'er the road we wheel.

"Are you all comfortable? Sit close as possible. Here we go! And now, on the road for home, let us be merry as we can be. Miss Pidgin, did you enjoy your duck?"—"You are a goose, sir, to talk so."—"Miss Primrose, you look refreshed since your sprinkling from nature's water-pot. Mr. Blisby, this is fine—a subject for a letter, Mr. Blisby. Jemima, my dear, you look as blooming as the rose in June, and twice as sweet. There's the Bozzleton factory rising above the trees, and the old vane, like vanity, pluming itself in the sunshine. Hurrah for home! Old lady with the mob-cap, take your head in doors. Urchins in corduroys, scatter. Young maiden with the milking-pail, *who* are you looking at?"

Mr. Blisby (rising).—"Before we part, I should like to say that the pleasure I have experienced has far exceeded my expectations, and that I shall always entertain a pleasing recollection of the delightful moments spent in this—in this—hay-cart!"

"Three cheers for Blisby! Ladies and gentlemen, if it is your opinion that we have enjoyed ourselves (a great way over the minister), you will please to manifest it. Yes! Then we'll adjourn with the chorus—

> "Some seek for glee by the heaving sea,
> Some rush on a railroad train,
> But give us a part on a country cart,
> And a pic-nic out in the rain!"
>
> *Exeunt Omnibus*, R. U. E.

AN EXCELLENT TEST OF AFFECTION.

"The summer is no time to try the strength of affection," said Mrs. Partington; "though it's pretty well to sing love songs beneath a window at midnight, in a rain-storm, or stand billing and cooing on the door-step till two o'clock in the morning. The winter season is the one. Many's the time my poor Paul has rid five miles to see me, the coldest weather; and often, the dear cretur has been found in the morning fast asleep in the middle of the cow-yard, with the saddle on his own shoulders, from fatigue with courting me, and riding a hard-trotting horse. There *was* devotion! I never see a cow without thinking of poor Paul;" and, saying which, the good old lady went to bed.

HIGH-DUTCH vs. POLITENESS.

"Has the Washington-street train gone by here?" asked Mrs. Partington of a gentleman with a huge moustache, who stood picking his teeth on the steps of the Revere House. The old lady meant the Washington-street omnibus that runs between the Lowell depôt and Dover-street. The gentleman still picked his teeth, and looked gravely at her, but said not a word. "Has the Washington-street train passed by here?" she asked again, thinking the gentleman hadn't heard her. He still stood, and stood still, and looked and picked, but said nothing. "Well!" said the old dame, half musing and half addressing the man with the moustache; "it was only a civil question, and I didn't think there was anything harmonious in asking it; but some people thinks it a great hardship to do any one a favour. It wouldn't have required much effort, I should think, to have answered me, nor took a great deal of anybody's time, nor interfered with anybody's occupancy. If anybody has got focal organs I should think they might use 'em."

"Nein ferstan," responded the man with the moustache, as he put his hands beneath his coat-tails, and walked up the steps, leaving Mrs. Partington standing like a note of interrogation at the end of her speech, while the omnibus, which had passed while she was speaking, was seen far in the distance.

GOOD TASTE.

"I can't bear children," said Miss Prim, disdainfully.

Mrs. Partington looked at her over her spectacles mildly before she replied.

"Perhaps if you could you would like them better," she at last said; "but why is it that unmarried old maids and single bachelors are always railing at children? It seems as if they had never read the command given to our forefathers to 'increase and multiply and punish the earth.' For my part, I love the little dears, and I had rather hear a child cry any day than hear the Brass Band."

And she went right to work covering a ball for Ike.

OLD ROGER MUCH EXCITED.

"Mrs. Timms," said old Roger, one morning, to his landlady at the breakfast-table; he was an old bachelor, was Roger, and, as such, was an object of considerable interest, both with the landlady and three antiquated spinsters who boarded with her. "Mrs. Timms, what sort of a house *do* you keep? What sort of a neighbourhood *is* this that you live in? and *why* is it that you have such a bad character round town, ma'am?"

The landlady was astonished, and well she might be, for he looked excited—incensed.

"I've boarded here, ma'am," continued he, "just seven weeks, and every week we have had a tract left here, and each tract is against some cardinal sin, ma'am, that you, nor me, nor the *young* ladies here, I *hope*, ever committed. Here's drunkenness, and gambling, and swearing, and lying, and stealing, and adultery, and bearing false witness,—almost all the sins in the church calendar, ma'am, and what 'll come next I can't guess. *I* can't stand it, ma'am. Why, the devil himself couldn't stand it."

And his brow looked hot and steamy, and he bore the look of a man injured by an implied reflection on a heretofore bright reputation.

RARE DUN.

ONE morning old Sledge got capsized out of his wherry, halibut and all, at the Spring Market, in P * * * * *, under the old dynastiness of that institution, and was nearly drowned when they got him out. He was so near death that the ones who caught him couldn't see any signs of life in him. But they rolled him and rubbed him and shook him, and sent off among the neighbours for warm blankets to put him in. Old Mrs. Twist, who lived on Church Hill, in the kindness of her heart, stripped her beds at once, and left her work all hanging, as she said, by "sixes and sevens," to go and help bring the man to. She warmed the blankets, and rubbed away vigorously at the inanimate Sledge, working as if her heart was in the operation, as undoubtedly it was. After a while, the rubbing took effect, or, as some suggested, his ugly nature refused to die, and he revived —slowly—slowly—first a gape and then a groan—then he opened his eyes, and the first person he looked upon was Mrs. Twist, busily enaged in her benevolent manipulations. He looked at her a moment, and consciousness returned.

"Ah!" said he, as he spit the salt-water out of his codlike mouth, " glad to see ye; been looking arter ye for a long time; would like to have ye pay me the two shillings ye owe me!"

Mrs. Twist assured us it was the most unthankfulest thing she ever heard of, and we think so too.

THE BEAR-SKINS.

"HERE come the sogers, aunt!" cried Ike, at the door, " here they come in their bear-skins!"

"In their bare skins!" said Mrs. Partington, glancing out of the window into the cold, towards the weathercock that had looked obstinately east for three days, much to the danger of a return of her rheumatism that an east wind always induced,—so much so that she had declared her determination to move in the vicinity of some Catholic church, whose vane always points one way,— " in their bare skins such a day as this! Highlanders, I guess."

She hastened to the door, and a company, with huge and hideous caps, were then marching by. She saw that she was sold.

"Ah!" said she, "this is one of the horrors of war, to go looking so; and s'pose one of them poor creatures should fall down,—he's so top-heavy his heels would go up in the air, like a cornstalk-witch, and all his brains would run down into his head. I can't bear to look at 'em."

She closed the door carefully, but she stood in the entry and beat time to the music till it had got far past the house.

A SLIGHT MISAPPREHENSION.

"How do you like the bustle and confusion of Boston?" asked the shop-keeper, as Mrs. Partington stood by the counter.

"It gives me confusion to see 'em," said the old lady; "folks didn't do so when I was a girl; and, besides, what an awful sight of bran and cotton it takes, to say nothing of their awkwardness when they get slipped on one side "—

"I mean," broke in the shopkeeper, "the bustle and confusion of the streets."

"O," said Mrs. P., "that is quite *another thing!*" and immediately left the store.

A REMEMBERED MISTAKE.

"It is all very true, Mr. Knickerbottom," said Mrs. Partington, as she read in the Knickerbocker something concerning brevity and simplicity of expression; "it's true, as you say; and how many mistakes there does happen when folks don't understand each other! Why, last summer I told a dressmaker to make me a long visite, to wear, and, would you believe it, she came and staid a fortnight with me? Since then I've made it a pint always to speak just what I say."

Her mouth grew down to a determined pucker at the end of the sentence, and the snuff-box was tapped energetically, as if the fortnight of unrequited bread and butter was lying heavily on her memory.

MRS. PARTINGTON AND JENNY LIND.

"I never liked the Swedenvirgins," said Mrs. Partington. She was orthodox, and always sat in the Asylum pew in the north-east corner of the gallery, and had charge of the children in sermon time. Her raised finger was an admonition that brought young refractories to their obedience at once. Every

K

Sunday was she there, and people expected to see the faded black
bonnet above the railings, in prayer-time, as much as they did the
parson. "I never liked the Swedenvirgins; but I a'n't one that
believes nothing good can come out of Lazarus, for all that. Now,
there's Jenny Lind,—may Heaven shower bags of gold on her
head!—that is so very good to everybody, and who sings so sweet
that everybody's falling in love with her, tipsy-turvy, and gives
away so much to poor, indignant people. They call her an angel,
and who knows but she may be a syrup in disguise, for the papers
say her singing is like the music of the spears. How I should
love to hear her!'

She grasped hastily at the long bead purse in her reticule, but
an unsatisfactory response came back from it to her hopes, and
she laid it back again with a sigh.

THE USE OF THE AZTECS.

"WE are fearfully and wonderfully made!" said Mrs. Partington, after she had stood for a long time contemplating the
Aztec children. Her hands were resting upon the back of a
chair as she said this, and she made the remark so loud that a
tall gentleman, who stood near her, stooped down to get a look
under her black bonnet. He thought she had spoken to him.
"We are fearfully and wonderfully made," continued she, "'spe-
cially some of us. The ways of Providence is past finding out,
and we don't know what these Haystack children are made for,
no more'n we do why the mermaids were made, or the man in the
moon. Perhaps they are made a purpose for curiosities, and nothing but Providence could make anything more so, unless Mr.
Barnum should try. Human natur never come done up in so
queer a wrapper before. They say they are distended from the
Haystacks long ago gone to grass. And Isaac," said she, turning
to Ike, who was teasing one of them with a stick, "Isaac, look
upon 'em, and pray you may never be born so."

The people had gathered around, and were listening to the
words as they fell, like the notes of a hand-organ, from her lips;
and when she ceased, they turned with renewed eagerness to inspect the objects that her remarks had rendered classic.

GOING TO CALIFORNIA.

"DRAB me!" exclaimed Mrs. Partington sorrowfully, "how
much a man will bear, and how far he will go, to get the soddered

·dross, as Parson Martin called it when he refused the beggar a
sixpence, for fear it might lead him into extravagance! Everybody is going to California and Chagrin arter gold. Cousin Jones
and the three Smiths have gone; and Mr. Chip, the carpenter,
has left his wife and seven children, and a blessed old mother-in-
law, to seek his fortin, too. This is the strangest yet, and I don't
see how he could have done it; it looks so ongrateful to treat
Heaven's blessings so lightly. But there, we are told that the
love of money is the root of all evil, and how true it is! for they
are now rooting arter it, like pigs arter groundnuts. Why, it is
a perfect money mania among everybody!"

And she shook her head doubtingly, as she pensively watched
a small mug of cider, with an apple in it, simmering by the winter fire. She was somewhat fond of drink made in this way.

A TOUGH CUSTOMER.

"WILL you help me to a piece of chicken?" asked Miss
Seraphima of old Roger, on Thanksgiving day. The old man
was engaged elbow-deep in the intricate task of carving; the perspiration stood upon his brow from his exertions,—truly Her-
culean efforts,—in dissecting a large fowl.

"Chicken!" muttered he; "do you call this a chicken? Why,
it has been the father of thousands, miss."

He hadn't a very thankful spirit that day, and the older boarders, with bad teeth, joined with him in questioning the propriety
of being thankful.

Old Roger's boarding-house having failed, and the furniture
being taken to be sold on *mean* process, as he called it, he asked
one of the chambermaids, who always had been saucy to him, if
she was to be sold with the rest of the furniture. She answered
him "No!" as sharp as vinegar.

"O," said he, coolly buttoning up his coat, "I supposed you
were, for the advertisement reads that the house is to be sold
with all the impertinences thereto belonging."

He very cruelly laughed at the indignant look she gave him,
and stepped out.

FUNERAL OBSTACLES.

"How solemn these funeral obstacles is!" said Mrs. Partington, as she looked down from an upper chamber window, on the

day of a mock funeral of one of the presidents. She took off her
specs to wipe the moisture from their discs, tapped her box
mournfully to the measured time of the distant drum, and looked
anxiously down the street, to catch the first glimpse of the funeral
train. "Here it comes at last," quoth she, "with the soldiers all
playing with muzzled drums, and their flags flying at half-mast.
Is that the catastrophe?" whispered she of a gentleman near her.

"That is the catafalque, madam," replied he.

"Well, well," said she, "no matter; I knowed there was a cat
about it, and I didn't know but it might be a cataplasm. Will
you tell me when the artillery flies over, that come on here to
tend the funeral?"

"Good gracious, madam!" cried he, testily, "they don't fly.
They are artillery men on horseback, merely."

"Dear me!" replied she, "I thought it was one of the wings
of the army, and flew. How easy it is to get mistaken!"

She pensively gazed upon the pageant that slowly passed
before her.

"What a pity it is," said she, "that we don't vally people
till arter they are dead; but then what paragorics we pour upon
them!"

She here paused; a silence pervaded the chamber; the procession had passed, the company had departed, and two hours
after the old lady was found still sitting by the open window fast
asleep. So powerful is grief!

EXCELLENT ADVICE.

"NEVER get in debt, Isaac," said Mrs. Partington; and she
raised her tea-spoon with an oracular air, and held it thus, as if
from it were suspended the threads of a fine argument on eco-
nomy, discernible to her eye alone, and she was watching an opportunity to make it tangible. "Never get in debt, no matter
whether you are creditable or not; it is better to live on a crust
of bread and water, and a herring or two, than cows and oxen cut
up into rump steaks, and owe for it. Think of our neighbour;
what a failing he had, and had all his goods and impertinences
took away on a mean procession and sold, and his poor wife re-
duced to a calico gound, starvation, and shushon tea, and he in
Californy!"

"Some tea, please," said Ike, as he handed over his tin dipper. The tea, like her own reflections, trickled out musically;
and she passed along the caution, with the cream and sugar,
never to get in debt.

PREPARING TO SEE THE PRESIDENT.

"MOTHER wants to know if you'll lend her a little merlasses to starch a cap, to go and see the President," said a little girl, coming into Mrs. Partington's kitchen, bearing in her hand a tin cup.

"Certainly, dear," said the good dame, pleasantly.

She never thought of the unreasonableness of the request; she never dreamed of guile. The treacle depository was brought out, the golden liquid filled the tin receptacle, and the child departed.

"Well!" said the old lady, "everybody is going to see the President. But what is a president, or a king, or a justice of the peace, but a man, arter all, with flesh and blood, and bones and hair, like any of us? And thousands will come further to see him than they would to see Saint Paul, or Hebrews, or Revelations, or any of 'em. Sich man-worship! sich man-worship!"

"The President's coming, aunt!" said Ike, bursting in; "and he's going by our door;" and the little fellow was half crazy with delight, and threw his cap in a pan of milk upon the table in his enthusiasm.

"How do I look, Isaac?" said the dame, with animation; "is my hair combed, and my handkerchief digested right on my neck, and my cap border even?" and she took her place by the window, when these questions were answered, as eager as any one to "see the President," and Ike stepped out. But her eyes were strangely dim, and those hitherto faithful specs gave indications now of failing her. She took them off to wipe them, and both glasses were gone! An hour before, Ike had borrowed them for a telescopic experiment. But it didn't make any odds, for the procession had turned down another street, and didn't go by her door at all.

A CHURCH INCIDENT.

THE bell had tolled for some minutes after the time of meeting, and some signs of impatience were manifest. A stranger, touching the occupant of a pew in front of him, asked, "Is your preacher often as late as this?"

"O, yes, sir," replied the interrogated; "it often happens that he don't get here till the sermon is half through!"

The stranger looked at him intently a little while, and then made a memorandum of this fact in his note-book.

A DRY-GOOD LESSON.

"Have you any stout dark marines?" said Mrs. Partington to the shopkeeper. He was one of these good-humoured young men, whose hair, nicely-curled, betokens an elegant taste, and he stood swaying back and forth, leaning on his yardstick, and smiled amiably as the old lady spoke. "Have you any dark marines, suitable for thick ladies' outside under garments?"

"We have dark moreens, ma'am," replied he, and cast his eyes towards a brother clerk, and winked archly. She gazed upon him a moment before she spoke again. "Well, well, young man, it was only a slip of the tongue; and if you never make a greater slip in measuring cloth, you will be much more honest than many clerks I know."

The clerk coloured and stammered out an apology, but it was needless. There was no unkindness in her looks. The spectacles bent their bows upon him steadily from the cavernous gloom of the big bonnet, but his perturbed fancy alone made them terrible. She made the purchase she intended, and in measure it praved full half a quarter over what she had bargained for.

A GLANCE AT POVERTY.

"It must be very inconvenient to be poor;" said Mrs. Partington, as she glanced with honest pride at her high-backed chairs and old-fashioned chest of drawers' and continued her eye on to the open cupboard in the corner. "How people can contrive to get along with so little, I don't see. There is our poor neighbour down the yard, now, is so pinched for room that she has to have a bed in the very room where she sleeps!"

Kind old lady! her benevolence walked ahead of her grammar; but a trifling error in speech is as pardonable in Mrs. Partington as in Henry Clay.

SLANDERERS.

"If there is anybody under the cannister of heaven that I have in utter excrescence," said Mrs. Partington, "it is a tale-bearer and slanderer, going about, like a vile boa-constructor, circulating his calomel about honest folks. I always know one by his phismahogany. It seems as if Beelzebub had stamped him with his private signal, and everything he looks at appears to turn yaller."

And, having uttered this somewhat elaborate speech, she was seized with a fit of coughing, and took some demulcent drops.

A STORMY SEASON.

"CEASE, rude Bolus, blustering railer!" said Mrs. Partington, as she reached out into the storm to secure a refractory shutter, and the wind rushed in and extinguished her light, and slammed to the door, and fanned the fire in the grate, and rustled the calico flounce upon the quilt, and peeped into the closet, and under the bed, and contemptuously shook Mrs. Partington's night-jacket, as it hung airing on the chair by the fire, and flirted with her cap-border, as she looked out upon the night. It was a saucy gust. "How it blows!" said she, as she shut down the window. "I hope Heaven will keep the poor sailors safe that go down on the sea in vessels! This must be the obnoxious storm," continued she, "when the sun crosses the Penobscot."

She donned her specs, and sat down to consult her almanac,—next to her Bible in importance,—and she found she was right, while the wind howled around the house most dismally, and yelled wildly down the old chimney.

DIETETICAL COUNSEL.

"You musn't be too greedy, Isaac," said Mrs. Partington, as, with an anxious expression, she marked a strong effort that young gentleman was making to achieve the last quarter of a mince-pie. "You shouldn't be so glutinous, dear. You must be careful, or you will get something in your elementary canal or sarcophagus one of these days, that will kill you, Isaac (she had been to hear a course of physiological lectures), and then you will have to be buried in the cold ground, and nobody won't never see you more; and what will I do, Isaac, when you are cut down in your priming, like a lovely jelly-flower?"

Much affected by the picture her own prolific fancy had conjured up, she pensively sweetened her tea for the fourth time, and looked earnestly upon Isaac, who, unheeding all she was saying, sat gazing at the street door, revolving in his mind the practicability of ringing the door-bell unperceived, without going outside.

MRS. P. CONFERS WITH PAUL.

"AND do you believe in the spiriteus knockings?" asked Mrs. Partington, as she leaned forward over the table, and bent her eyes on a queer individual who had related some wonderful things he had seen. "O, I would like to have poor Paul come back!"

A gentle rapping upon the old chest in the corner attracted

their attention, and the whole of them immediately surrounded it.

"If it's Paul's apprehension," said Mrs. Partington, "I know
he'll answer me. Paul, is that you?"

Knock.

"Just like him," said she, smiling, "when he was living, he
was always tapping when he had anything in the house to tap.
Didn't you, Paul?"

Knock.

"Can't you speak to me?"

Knock.

"Does that mean yes or no?"

Knock.

"Which does it mean?"

Knock.

Some of the party suggested that the alphabet should be called,
which was done.

"Are you in want of anything?" said she.

Knock.

"What is it?"

And the anxious spectators, through the medium of the alphabet, spelled out "S-i-d-u-r."

"It is Paul!" cried the old lady, delightedly; "that's the
way he always spelled it. Do you want me to come to you,
Paul?"

The answer came back, "No, I'm in better company!"

The old lady turned away mournfully. There was sorrow in
the wavy lock of gray that straggled beneath her cap border,—
there was a quaver of grief in the tone that inquired for the scis-
sors,—there was a misty vapour upon her specs, like the dew
upon the leaves after rain,—the cap-border, like a flag at half-
mast, trailed in woe over the ruin of disappointed affection. At
that instant the cover of the chest opened, and the head of Ike,
protruding, disclosed the secret of the knockings.

"Ah, you rogue!" said she, a smile dispelling all evidence of
disorder, "Ah, you rogue! was it you? You'll never be a good
spirit as long as you live, I'm afraid, if you go on so. But I
knowed it wasn't Paul!"

There was triumph in her tone, and it seemed as if a whole
basketful of sunshine had been upset in that room, it was so
pleasant all the rest of the evening.

THE END

Printed by BoD™in Norderstedt, Germany